A Theory of
Japanese Democracy
Nobutaka Ike

Westview Press • Boulder, Colorado

Dawson • Folkestone, England

This volume is included in Westview's Special Studies on China and East Asia.

Copyright © 1978 by Westview Press, Inc.

Published in 1978 in the United States of America by
  Westview Press, Inc.
  5500 Central Avenue
  Boulder, Colorado 80301
  Frederick A. Praeger, Publisher and Editorial Director

Published in 1978 in Great Britain by
  Wm. Dawson and Sons, Ltd.
  Cannon House
  Folkestone
  Kent CT19 5EE

Library of Congress No.: 77-8279
ISBN (U.S.): 0-89158-066-2
ISBN (U.K.): 0-7129-0817-X

Printed and bound in the United States of America

A Theory of
Japanese Democracy

A Theory of Japanese Democracy
Nobutaka Ike

In this book Nobutaka Ike, long concerned with the problem of Japanese democracy, proposes a model of the Japanese democratic system. It is a rational choice model modified somewhat to correspond to Japanese empirical data; it is also an investment model that likens politicians to entrepreneurs and voters to investors. Voters support certain politicians or coalitions of politicians—political parties— and in return expect different benefits. They can register their support individually or by forming consortia.

In the first part of the book Professor Ike develops his theory, which is illustrated and elaborated on in the second part with empirical data drawn from election returns, survey research data, and specialized monographs.

Professor Ike asserts that the political change of recent decades may be explained succinctly by the use of his model. Through it he demonstrates that the kinds of benefits sought by voters have been changing because of economic growth and urban migration, and that the democratic system has been slow to adapt to new demands.

Nobutaka Ike is professor of political science at Stanford University. He has held visiting professorships in universities in the United States, Japan, and the Philippines and has received fellowships for travel and research in Japan from the Ford Foundation, the Social Science Research Council, the Rockefeller Foundation, and the Japan Foundation. His numerous publications include *Japanese Politics: Patron-Client Democracy* and *Japan, the New Superstate*.

To Tai

Contents

41327

Tables and Figures

Tables

xi

Figures

Preface

In 1973 Peter Berton invited me to speak at one of the seminar meetings of a group of Japan specialists residing in Southern California. At this particular meeting, which was held at San Diego State University, I presented some of my preliminary ideas on a theory of Japanese democracy and sought the advice of those present as to whether, in their view, it would be worthwhile for me to go on with the project. To my relief, the seminar participants gave me encouragement—for which I wish to thank them. Later in the fall of 1973, I spent some seven weeks in Tokyo to confer with Japanese political scientists and to collect data. The trip was made possible in part by the Japan Foundation, and I wish to indicate my appreciation for the financial assistance it gave me. During the Christmas holidays in 1976, I made another trip to Tokyo, this time to study the December 1976 election for the House of Representatives and to collect the material I needed to bring the manuscript up to date.

During these two trips, a number of individuals gave me help and encouragement and extended their hospitality to my wife and me. I wish in particular to acknowledge my indebtedness to Professor Kyogoku Jun-ichi, Makoto Saito, Seki Hiroharu, Ukai Nobushige, Konno Genpachiro, Inoki

Masamichi, Higuchi Tokihiro, Hosoya Chihiro, Nakamura Hajime, Mr. Arai Makoto, and Mr. and Mrs. Joe Ike. I would also like to thank Dr. Hayashi Chikio, of the Institute of Mathematical Statistics, for making some of his works available. I am especially grateful to Mr. Kohei Shinsaku, of the Public Opinion Research Institute of the Japan Broadcasting Corporation, for providing me with his numerous studies of Japanese electoral behavior and with opportunities to discuss problems of mutual interest. Mr. Naito Takeshi and Mr. Hagiwara Michihiko, of Tokyo Shimbun, were also helpful.

The Faculty of Law at the University of Tokyo generously appointed me a visiting foreign research scholar and thereby greatly facilitated my work in Tokyo. I wish also to thank the staff of the International House of Japan for the courtesies they extended to me. As usual, the staff of the Japanese Collection of the Hoover Institution at Stanford University have gone out of their way to be helpful to me.

Several of my colleagues—Professors Kurt Steiner, Heinz Eulau, and Daniel Okimoto—read all or parts of earlier drafts of the manuscript and gave me the benefit of their comments. Of course, I alone am responsible for any errors and shortcomings that may remain. The editorial staff of Westview Press, and in particular Mervyn Seldon, have been most helpful in improving the final draft of the manuscript. Finally, I wish to thank my wife for her help in proofreading and numerous chores connected with the publication of the book, and Brian Ike for providing me with press reports on the results of the 1977 House of Councillors election.

Nobutaka Ike
October 3, 1977
Stanford University

Introduction

This book, like many others, has an intellectual history of its own. In an earlier work (*Japanese Politics: Patron-Client Democracy, 1972*), I suggested that a patron-client model of democracy would be appropriate for understanding and explaining Japanese politics but was unable to present such a model in detail, partly because my thoughts on it had not yet crystallized sufficiently, and partly because the subject lay somewhat outside of the scope of the book, which stressed political structure and processes in contemporary Japan.

But I continued to be interested in trying to work out a model of Japanese democracy, however crude and rudimentary it might be. I was stimulated to do so to some extent by a growing conviction that some of the empirical democratic theories being proposed and debated in the current political science literature would produce anomalous results when applied to Japanese politics.

By way of illustration, I can cite two fairly recent examples. Bradley Richardson has made a detailed analysis of the relationship between urbanization and political participation. He found that the data he had assembled on Japanese urbanization ran contrary both to Daniel Lerner's prediction that urbanization will lead to greater political participation, with education and mass media development acting as intervening variables, and to Karl Deutsch's well-known model of social mobilization. "Japan," Richardson wrote, "is one of the important examples of a country in which urban residence and political participation are negatively correlated."[1] To explain the deviation from what empirical theory had predicted, he cited a number of factors, including community structure, political culture, communications and administrative networks, social structure, group membership, economic interest, and sectoral differences. What Richardson did was to suggest ad hoc reasons as to why the theory and empirical data did not fit. He did not propose an alternative model that would explain the Japanese data in a parsimonious fashion.

The second example is a study Chong Lim Kim undertook using data drawn from Japanese prefectures. His object was to test theories proposed by Seymour M. Lipset, Phillips Cutright, and others relating socioeconomic development to political democracy. These theories have to do with comparing different nations at different stages in their development, but Kim applied the theories to prefectures within one nation, Japan. He developed a series of indicators on urban industrialism and social overhead (automobiles, roads, newspapers, electric power, libraries) and related these two dimensions to other indicators showing the degree of democracy, that is, party competition, political participation, and equality of representation. His conclusion was that the generalizations reported in the cross-national studies were not confirmed by internal Japanese data. "The findings presented here," Kim wrote, "suggest that socioeconomic factors such as the level of urbanization, industrialization, education, or communications development provide an inadequate explanation for the varying levels of political democracy in Japanese prefectures."[2]

These and other examples that can be found in the literature persuaded me that it might be worthwhile to try to develop a model of Japanese democracy that would help explain a variety of contemporary Japanese political phenomena. For example, the investment model that will be proposed in this book would seem to explain what Richardson noted, namely, a lower rate of political participation in urban areas than in rural areas. This model would also suggest why the ruling Liberal Democratic party has steadily lost voter support despite its success in managing the nation's economy in such a way as to produce unprecedented growth, why the opposition parties have developed a strong following in the big cities, why social class as an explanatory variable in politics is often rather limited, and why localism persists in certain sections of the country.

Furthermore, the investment model might be useful from a broader comparative perspective. A growing number of cross-national studies are focused on particular aspects of political systems. Gabriel Almond and Sidney Verba have studied political culture comparatively across five nations,[3] and Giovanni Sartori has analyzed political parties in a large number of nations.[4] These efforts have produced valuable generalizations and enriched the body of empirical theory available to political scientists. It occurred to me that we also ought to be able to study democratic models comparatively. For instance, if we had models of Japanese, American, French, German, British, Italian, Filipino, Indian, and other democracies, we might be able to come up with some interesting generalizations about democratic politics. At least that is my hope, and the present work is intended to be a modest effort to stimulate thinking and writing along these lines.

Finally, the investment model belongs in the general category of "rational choice" models, which rest on the fundamental assumption that human beings make rational choices when acting politically. As will become evident, I have made some modifications in the conventional model in order to take into account certain features that stand out in

Japanese politics, features such as social relations based on vertical society with its small group orientation and dependency feelings.

Part 1 consists of three chapters that are intended to delineate a theory of Japanese democracy and the background factors, such as social structure, that enter into such a theory. Part 2 contains four chapters that are more empirical in approach. It would be too presumptuous to say that they are supposed to test the model outlined in part 1. Rather, they should be viewed as attempts to illustrate and in some cases to elaborate on themes developed in part 1. Chapters 4 and 5 stress the need to take social networks into account in trying to explain cleavages and changes in party support. Chapter 6 is a foray into urban politics, a subject of increasing concern and interest. This is followed by chapter 7, which considers the pull that localism based on personal considerations exerts in Japanese politics. Chapter 8 seeks to apply the investment model to recent political change.

A Theory of
Japanese Democracy

Part 1
A Theory of Japanese Democracy

1
The Market Model of Democracy

As a concept, democracy is not without its ambiguities. It is sometimes used in a normative sense. When applied in this way, it refers to an ideal, a polity and society characterized by a high degree of personal freedom, social and economic equality, and self-government; that is, a polity and society that permit wide participation in the political process. In modern nation-states, the ideal generally cannot be obtained in practice. Modern democracy does not involve direct participation in the decision-making process to any great extent; rather, it delegates power to a political elite, that is, it rests on the principle of representation.

Thus, democracy is associated with representative government, in which governing elites are somehow supposed to be responsive to the needs and demands of citizens and accountable to them. This responsiveness and accountability may be obtained by certain procedural and structural arrangements, such as free elections and institutional checks and balances. At the minimum, democracy is a way of choosing and legitimizing government. It is a system in which voters collectively choose one or more groups of party politicians who compete for electoral support given in free elections in order to gain control of the government until the next election. The Japanese political system since 1945 certainly meets this test.

But some theorists of democracy have argued that it involves more than just a technique of government.[1] Behind the demand that voters collectively choose the government must lie some basic assumptions about human nature. There must be something about human beings that justifies having a government that depends on collective judgments rendered by the people. In Western democracies there is a certain conception of the individuals who make up the political system. It is often believed that every individual possesses innate capabilities and that these capabilities ought to be developed as fully as possible. It is believed further that a democratic society provides the best medium through which these capabilities can be developed, because capabilities ought to be developed under one's conscious control rather than at the dictate of another. It is probably in this sense that freedom and equality have been long considered essential in Western democratic theory, for without freedom and equality individuals cannot fully develop their capabilities.

The situation in Japan is somewhat different. Analysts of Japanese culture and society have pointed to the need for achievement that many Japanese exhibit. There is a strong competitive strain in Japanese culture, which is perhaps best exemplified by the spectacle of countless youth dedicating their adolescent years to intensive study in preparation for the college and university entrance examinations. Thus, like Americans, Japanese also believe that individuals have capabilities that ought to be developed. But in the West, the stress has been on self-realization in individualistic terms; in Japan it has been defined in social group terms. Thus, as George De Vos has noted, "The ideal found in the West of self-realization apart from family and social group has been entirely alien to the Japanese system of thought (outside that of a small group of intellectuals) until very recently."[2]

Thus individuals in Japan are encouraged to develop their capabilities not as an end in itself, but to contribute more to the good of the family or group and, by extension, quite possibly to society. Conceivably, one could take the position that only democracy based on individualism, the democracy found in the West, is genuine, but such a view would be rather ethnocentric. There seems to be no good reason to exclude Japan from the list of democratic nations that exist in the world today. But one would also anticipate that Japanese democracy would not necessarily reproduce all of the features of Western democracies; its social and cultural basis is different. In any case, although I am not completely indifferent to the normative aspects of democracy, it is not the main concern of this book. I do not wish to debate the pros and cons of whether Japan is a democracy in the sense in which the term is understood. It seems to me that the minimum requirements are met, and I am willing to go on from there.

The concept of democracy may also be used in an empirical sense. Here the emphasis falls on what is rather than on what ought to be. Empirical theory seeks to explain as well as describe how a democratic political system operates. Different kinds of propositions can be advanced that, in the form of hypotheses, state relationships that are thought to obtain between different kinds of political phenomena; such propositions can then be tested empirically against the data. Propositions about the relationship between urbanization and political participation cited earlier are an example. In this book, I propose to concentrate on empirical democratic theory.

There are several "models" of democracy from which one may draw different propositions about democratic politics. A model is a simplified representation of reality, one that posits a limited number of elements and specifies the relationship among these elements. A good model should help explain as well as predict the political phenomena that are being observed.

The Market Model

The market model has occupied an influential position in American political science in recent years. As the name implies, the model takes the democratic political system to be roughly analogous to the competitive market system. Economic analysis starts with the assumption that individuals are rational and selfish and seek to maximize gains (or minimize real costs). As consumers, they try to buy goods as cheaply as possible. But as producers or sellers, they seek to get as high a price as possible in order to maximize profits. Buyers and sellers get together when they can agree on the price at which the transaction will take place. According to economic analysis, then, both sellers and buyers, acting out of purely selfish motives, benefit from the economic exchange involved in transactions.

Moreover, the economic system, according to classical economic theory, is self-adjusting. If consumers believe that prevailing prices are too high, they will presumably cut down on their purchases. When this happens, goods that are being manufactured will begin to pile up in warehouses, and sellers will be forced to lower prices in order to stimulate demand. Producers will also reduce production schedules until demand and supply come into balance. So the economic system, with the help of the price mechanism, always moves in the direction of equilibrium, even though at the micro level individual consumers and producers are acting out of selfish motives. As C. B. Macpherson notes, "The economist has been able to show how the results of countless separate decisions by individual producers and consumers could be a determinate system."[3]

Following classical economic theory, the market model of democratic politics also postulates that rational and selfish individuals act to promote their self-interest. Thus, in his famous and often-quoted *An Economic Theory of Democracy*, Anthony Downs states that "we assume that every individual, though rational, is also selfish."[4] In democratic politics individuals will promote their self-interest by seeking to maximize benefits flowing from the government. According to Downs, "All citizens are constantly receiving streams of benefits from government activities. Their streets are policed, water purified, roads repaired, shores defended, garbage removed, weather forecast, etc."[5] Individuals as recipients of benefits may be likened to consumers.

The equivalent of the producers or sellers would be the politicans who seek election to public office. Downs assumes that politicians are motivated purely by selfish goals, that is, they seek "income, prestige, and power," which comes from being in office. "Thus politicians in our model never seek office as a means of carrying out particular policies; their only goal is to reap the rewards of holding office per se. They treat policies purely as means to the attainment of their private ends, which they can reach only by being elected."[6]

Politicians, moreover, are organized into teams, that is, political parties. Downs further assumes that all party members "agree on all their goals instead of on just part of them," which means that a party may be likened to a single person, a somewhat unrealistic assumption.[7]

In the democratic political model, as in the economic model, voters (consumers) interact with politicians or teams of politicians (producers). What is lacking is a price mechanism that intervenes to influence the behavior of consumers and producers seeking to maximize their self-interest. The closest analogy is political support. Thus Downs notes, "Our model is based on the assumption that every government seeks to maximize political support."[8] In order to attain this goal, the government must "discover some relationship between what it does and how citizens vote."[9] Since citizens seek to maximize benefits, Downs argues that each person votes "for the party he believes will provide him with more benefits that any other."[10] As a result, the

government adopts policies that produce the most votes.
Thus politicians, whose primary interest in securing public
office is private gain, should end up adopting policies that
maximize benefits for the voters, that is, perform a useful
social function.[11] Indeed, they even try to get voters to believe
that their policies are best for the voters.[12]

Political support is also an important element in David
Easton's well-known analysis of political systems. In Easton's view, there is a scarcity of some valued things, and politics involves the struggle over the allocation of these scarce
values. Like Downs, he seems to make the basic assumption
that individuals seek to maximize their acquisition of scarce
values.[13]

In seeking to acquire scarce values, individuals and
groups of individuals make demands on the decision-
makers. These demands are "inputs" in Easton's view, and
the public policies and actions that result are "outputs." If
the authorities are to build political support, they must be
able to match the outputs to the demands that have been
made, and this involves having information about the
amount of political support they are getting from the
citizens and the effects the current outputs will have on this
support. Information, in other words, enables citizens and
decision-makers to adjust to each other, and in this sense, it
appears to function somewhat like the price mechanism in
the economic system.[14]

Acquiring information invariably involves some cost,
however. For instance, voters who seek to choose rationally
the political party that will presumably bring them most
benefits will need to do some research on the performance of
political parties in the past and make some judgments as to
their likely performance in the future. Moreover, a voter's
calculations must include the possibility that his or her vote
will represent the margin between victory or defeat for the
political party he or she favors. If the conclusion is that the
one vote is not likely to affect the outcome, then a rational

person will not vote, because the party the voter favors will win in any case without the voter incurring any costs.

Furthermore, even if voters can acquire different kinds of information, they may not necessarily make the right decision. Life is full of uncertainties. Downs suggests a number of ways in which voters, for example, can reduce information costs and uncertainty, but in the end he concludes that it is irrational to be politically well informed because of the costs involved.[15]

As can be seen, this kind of cost-benefit analysis paints a highly simplified picture of reality, yet, interestingly enough, it can help explain various kinds of phenomena one encounters in the real world of politics. For instance, it suggests why a substantial number of voters may decide to stay at home when the weather is bad on election day. They may be convinced that the costs of voting under those circumstances outweigh the benefits they would receive, since their vote is hardly likely to affect the outcome. By the same token, Downs's model predicts that in closely contested electoral battles, where the outcome is perceived to be in doubt, the voting rate is likely to be higher than normal. This prediction is likely to be borne out in many cases.

At the same time, the model has some shortcomings. It does not explain adequately why some voters persist in voting for small opposition parties that have no chance of winning an election. According to Downs's theory, such action is irrational, yet obviously supporters of minor opposition parties do not agree with that interpretation. Peter Blau has suggested that politics involves more than a calculation of advantage; it also includes feelings of antagonism toward those in power, or a sense of alienation from the system.[16]

An even more serious weakness has to do with the fact that so many people in most political systems do take the trouble to vote. Downs's model explains why some people might choose not to vote, but it does not tell us why so many do. Downs attempts to get around this difficulty with the explanation that "one thing that all citizens in our model have in common is the desire to see democracy work."[17] So, according to this line of reasoning, an individual "is willing to bear certain short-run costs he could avoid in order to do his share in providing long-run benefits."[18] As some critics have pointed out, this argument greatly weakens the deductive power of the economic model, because now the analysis has shifted from individual costs and benefits to the collective interest. Voting to do "one's share" in maintaining the democratic system and thereby bring long-run benefits is quite a different matter from acting to promote one's self-interest on the basis of rational calculations of the costs and benefits one obtains from the act of going to the polls.[19]

The Investment Model, a Variant

Recently, an "investment model," which may be looked upon as variant of the market model, has been proposed by Samuel Popkin et al. Specifically, the model seeks to explain what has been happening in American politics during the last twenty years or so, but with some modifications (to be suggested later), it would appear to be useful for looking at contemporary Japanese politics as well.[20]

This variant model views the voter as an "investor" rather than as a consumer. Popkin et al. do not characterize party politicians in any way, but I would liken them to "entrepreneurs." Thus the basic actors in this model are investors putting their capital, which in this case consists of votes and other forms of political support, into the hands of entrepreneurs in exchange for anticipated returns on their investment. As Popkin states, this assumes an instrumental view of politics: we "will propose a view of voting that sees the voter as an investor and characterizes each vote as *an investment in one or more collective goods made under conditions of uncertainty with costly and imperfect information.*"[21]

Because labor is costly and imperfect in this model, voters make use of "partisan and ideological labels" in an effort to cut down information costs.[22] Such costs also affect the degree of political involvement because investor-voters weigh potential returns against costs. Since cost-return ratios can be expected to vary depending on one's political situation and other factors, the investor model "predicts that involvement will vary as the voter's life situation changes and as he responds to new opportunities and political events."[23]

It is evident that political outputs are important, whether we look at voters as consumers or as investors. An instrumental view of politics would lead one to pay particular attention to the stream of benefits expected to flow from governmental activity. It is customary, as Popkin et al. do, to regard such benefits as "collective goods."

Collective goods are sometimes referred to as "indivisible benefits." This is because collective goods, once provided, are available to everyone, whether or not an individual has paid for them. A typical example is national defense. All citizens benefit from it even though some have paid high taxes and others have paid none at all. A second, and less important, characteristic of collective goods is that the supply is not diminished regardless of how many people enjoy the benefits. Many of the outputs of the political system are collective goods.

But government action also leads to "divisible benefits," that is, benefits that accrue to a subset of the population rather than to everyone. For example, a public park directly benefits those people who live near it and use it frequently but not those who live farther away from it and never leave home.[24]

I would add a third category of benefits, which for lack of a better term I will call political party patronage. What I have in mind are benefits provided by quasi-public bodies such as political parties. For example, in Japan the religious organization Sokagakkai provides a whole array of benefits for its members—a sense of belonging, economic security, status, the opportunity to participate in organized activities, and so on. The Sokagakkai is closely associated with the Komeito or Clean Government party, and it is not surprising that large numbers of Sokagakkai members support Komeito candidates in elections. To a lesser extent, this is also true of the Communist party in recent years. It provides all kinds of benefits to members and supporters, especially in the large cities where it has succeeded in building up strong support.[25]

The fourth and final category of benefits would be "individual benefits." Governments do deal with people on an individual basis. For instance, government agencies hire people, thereby providing employment opportunities. Government agencies also issue licenses and building permits, let contracts, and the like. To the extent that individuals are able to get preferential treatment through the use of political leverage, there are individual benefits to be gained from government.

The basic assumption of the investment model is that citizens invest in political entrepreneurs hoping for some kind of returns or benefits, whether indivisible or otherwise. The voters are exchanging political support for political outputs. As stated before, the model assumes an instrumental approach to politics. This model would seem to fit the Japanese case, for as Richardson and others have shown, instrumental attitudes are quite prevalent among Japanese voters.[26]

2
Social Networks and Vertical Society

The market model rests on certain assumptions about what motivates individuals to behave as they do. It assumes that individuals seek to maximize their gains and minimize their losses, that is, that they are bent on promoting their self-interest. It treats individuals as discrete entities functioning in relative isolation, and it does not have as an explanatory variable the effects individuals have on each other as they interact (except as producers and consumers or investors and entrepreneurs.)

In recent years, some concern has been expressed about the failure to incorporate social interaction data in analyzing political phenomena, especially voting behavior. An article by Carl Sheingold, a sociologist, has called for more research on the impact of social networks on individual voting decisions and on the flow of information and influence through society as a whole. It further suggests that in the 1940s and 1950s the Columbia school of researchers began work on social networks but was superseded by the Michigan group, which focused more on political attitudes held by individuals as a predictor of voting behavior and on the effect voter behavior in the aggregate has had on partisan divisions within the electorate as it has responded to changes in public policy. In this article, Sheingold calls for a return to the earlier tradition of a more sociological orientation.[1]

It is true that earlier studies on voting decisions paid considerable attention to the existence of social networks. For example, in *Voting: A Study of Opinion Formation in a Presidential Campaign,* Bernard R. Berelson, Paul F. Lazarsfeld, and William N. McPhee noted how friends and coworkers "serve less as closed cliques than as contact points through whom the individual is connected to whole networks of social relations that affect political behavior."[2] Moreover, social networks can provide diverse information, competing ideas, aggregate experience, and collective judgments and in this way affect the political choices an individual makes. Thus, if those within one's social networks have rather homogeneous political views, it is likely that one's convictions about a candidate will be strong. By contrast, if a person's immediate social environment is split in political preference, that individual is more likely to be influenced by the majority in the larger community.[3]

Berelson also pointed out, however, that although "friends are responsive to other friends in chains running through thousands of people, " there are limits to how these networks extend. As a result, there is not just one social network, but many. Therefore, "there is not just 'one' community of continuously connected groups and therefore of uniform political discussion in Elmira [the community Berelson studied] but a number of only partly integrated subcommunities."[4]

Despite the concern that researchers of the Columbia school had for social interaction, they did not collect data that relate directly to how information and influence flow through social networks—as Sheingold noted. Sheingold therefore proposed new research endeavors to clarify the effect of social structure on political choice.[5]

Other scholars have expressed similar sentiments. For example, a British study focuses on the effect of neighborhood structure on voting behavior. Its author, Martin Fitton, argues that "it could be hypothesized that all correlations relating to voting behavior developed without adequate control of interactional variables must necessarily be of little use; they may allow prediction but cannot provide explanation."[6]

Another study—by Paul Burstein using Israeli data—states that "the influence of friends and relatives on political choice is likely to be stronger than the effects of background variables because the payoffs from interpersonal influence are more immediate and tangible than payoffs related to other variables."[7] Burstein found not only that direct and indirect social ties to political parties, ties "operating through little groups of friends, relatives, and the people they know," had an independent effect on party choice, but also that such social network ties intervened between background variables and the vote.[8]

More recently, Heinz Eulau has also proposed that data on social networks be collected for the study of electoral behavior. He suggests that survey research has sought to explain and predict the way in which the individual voter behaves, and "through such explanation and prediction [has also tried to] explain and predict collective electoral outcomes."[9] By so doing, it has neglected the impact of social interaction on political behavior.

"In the social network perspective, then, collective choice is not simply a matter of arithmetically computing declared preferences of individuals but a product that emerged out of interactions among persons who are related to each other as family members, friends, neighbors, work associates, and so on."[10] Accordingly, Eulau sees the social network as intervening between "antecedent stimuli (which may be long- or short-term) and the formal voting act of the person."[11]

Needless to say, new research methodologies have to be used to get at this dimension. Eulau wonders, for example, whether whole social units—families, work groups, street blocks—should be interviewed. Another possible method is snowball sampling, in which respondents are asked to name one or more friends or associates; the persons thus named are then interviewed.

My purpose in reviewing recent proposals for bringing in social networks as an important variable in political research is to suggest that if this is important for understanding and explaining American electoral politics, it is even more important when dealing with Japanese politics. In Japan, despite social change wrought by modernization and Westernization, the individualism that is such an integral part of Western culture is not widely found. As has been frequently noted, there is an unmistakable group orientation in Japanese social life. It is to this subject that we now turn.

Vertical Society

Chie Nakane's theory of Japanese society provides us with a convenient point of departure. She has used the term *vertical* (*tate* in Japanese) to characterize the social structure in Japan. In her view, "the most characteristic feature of Japanese social organization arises from the single bond in social relationships: an individual or a group has always one single distinctive relation to the other."[12] That relationship is one of inequality, which leads to hierarchy. "The ranking order which produces delicate differentiations between members of a group develops firm personal links between superior and subordinate."[13]

What Nakane is describing may be called (as in anthropological literature) a dyad, which represents a two-person interactional model. Dyads have certain properties. For example, they are based on individual ties rather than on shared characteristics, such as a belief in a common religion or political ideology. Dyadic relationships, moreover, involve direct social exchange of favors of mutual benefit. These social exchanges serve to strengthen bonds of friendship and loyalty and to establish a superordination-subordination relationship.

Dyads can be expanded so that the person in the superior position can have more than one subordinate, as in figure 2-1. The A-B, A-C grouping can also grow further with subordinates B and C acting as subleaders, as in figure 2-2.

Figure 2-1

Obviously figure 2-2 depicts a "group," but unfortunately the English language does not distinguish this kind of group from other groups that do not have these characteristics. For the lack of a better term, I will arbitrarily call what is depicted in figure 2-2 as a dyadic group; when the term *group* is used in the discussion that follows, it refers to a dyadic group.

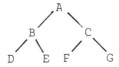

Figure 2-2

This kind of social structure, by the way, is not unique to Japan. Something similar is found in many parts of Asia and in parts of southern Europe, such as Italy and Greece. The general term used to characterize this phenomenon is *patron-client system* or *political clientelism*. There is as yet no good theory of clientelism, but the literature on the subject is growing.[14]

In the case of Japan, one may think of its society as being made up of a series of small, informal groups consisting of a dozen to two dozen individuals. Every individual has a group to which he is most devoted. Groups are important in that they provide individuals with a sense of social identity. Group membership, moreover, helps to meet emotional and affective needs and heightens one's sense of security. Within the group, solidarity is stressed, with the result that individual autonomy is minimized.

Group members, as indicated above, are organized vertically in a delicate and intricate ranking system based fundamentally on seniority. "Without consciousness of ranking, life could not be carried on smoothly in Japan," notes Nakane, "for rank is the social norm on which Japanese life is based."[15] The highest rank, of course, is held by the leader who helps to hold the group together. The effective leader in an organization, for example, is one who is able to establish highly personalized and emotional ties with his subordinates. His dealings with his followers are characterized by a high degree of paternalism, and above all he must be concerned with the welfare of his subordinates. "The emotional sympathy felt by the leader towards his subordinates is expressed in the term, *onjo-shugi*, or 'paternalism' and always presupposes a sympathetic appreciation for his men."[16] A person who is unable to "capture" his followers emotionally, according to Nakane, cannot become a leader, and she speculates that this may explain why Japan does not have charismatic leaders and that a leader's charisma, if expressed at all, is only "through immediate personal relations."[17]

In return for paternalistic leadership, the followers are obligated to show loyalty and devotion to the leader and to the group. "Action should be always for the group, not calculated in terms of the individual."[18] It is not surprising, under the circumstances, that relationships among group members can be intense and that such relationships can embrace virtually the totality of a person's life. Members "of a group know each other exceedingly well—one's family, love affairs, even the limits of one's capacity for cocktails are intimately known to the others. "[19] The maintenance of such close relationships necessitates, of course, that group members be in frequent face-to-face contact with each other. The more often people interact, the closer the bond is likely to be.

The obverse of strong in-group feelings is indifference or even latent hostility to outsiders. A distinction is often made between "we" and "they." Most Japanese find it difficult to relate to people they do not know, and this is why they prefer to get introductions from a third party when they find it necessary to have dealings with a stranger. In effect, individuals cannot move easily from one group to another. Thus it is difficult for Japanese to form and maintain effective voluntary organizations because such organizations are not likely to be structured on the vertical principle.[20] After all, it is the very nature of voluntary associations to be made up of people of diverse backgrounds who come together for functional and rather limited purposes.

I do not wish to imply that voluntary organizations do not exist in Japan. They do, and their numbers are probably growing. The important point is that such organizations tend to have a diffuse structure, to become fragmented through fission, and to have difficulty in uniting in the pursuit of common goals.

By the same token, the awareness of social class is not highly developed. As Nakane puts it, "The overall picture of society resulting from such inter-personal (and inter-group) relations is not that of horizontal stratification by class or caste but of vertical stratification by institution or group of institutions."[21] To put it another way, corporations made up of managers and workers compete with other corporations, but workers as a class generally do not see themselves as pitted against a capitalist class.

If Japanese society is indeed more sharply stratified along vertical than horizontal lines, then we may ask what holds the groups together. The answer appears to be that there must be some kind of framework within which groups are able to operate. The existence of this framework makes it possible for small groups to cooperate and coordinate their activities. An example of such a framework is an institution, such as a university (more details will be provided in chapter 3). Nakane believes that the more prestigious and important the institution, when compared to others like it, the more coherence group members will exhibit. This is because the stronger institutions have more centralized communications systems and have greater capacity to mobilize group members for the attainment of institutional goals.

The most comprehensive and in many ways the most important framework, of course, is the state. If Japanese society is looked upon as an aggregation of competing and even latently hostile groups that find it difficult of their own accord to establish meaningful links with one another, then the importance of the central administration as a coordinating and directing agency can be readily appreciated. Once the various small groups accept the authority of the state, its commands can be easily transmitted through the vertical organizational structure.[22]

That a centralized bureaucratic adminstration is necessary if Japanese society is to be coordinated and integrated does not necessarily mean that its authority will be received gratefully and gracefully. On the contrary, submission to authority is usually accompanied by suspicion, fear, and hostility. As Nakane notes, obedience in Japanese culture takes the form of "total submission," and "any criticism of or opposition to authority tends to be seen as heroism."[23]

The reason for this all-or-nothing stance, I would speculate, is to be found in the dynamics of the decision-making process. Within the vertically organized small groups, decisions are not made unilaterally by the leader but represent a consensus in which rank-and-file members have had opportunities to make significant inputs. But in the case of orders emanating ultimately from governmental agencies, most people have not had such opportunities, and they may therefore resent authoritative commands coming from above.

Psychological Attitudes

The principle of social organization based on vertical ties finds its counterpart in individual Japanese psychology. Here we turn to the concept of *amae* as articulated by Takeo Doi, a practicing psychiatrist.[24] On the basis of his psychiatric practice as well as his study of Western psychological theory, Doi has put forward the theory that *amae* may be regarded as the key concept in understanding Japanese social structure, and he explicitly states that it is consonant with Nakane's idea of a vertical society. Actually, one might look upon vertical society and *amae* as two sides of the same coin.

Stated simply, Doi's *amae* has to do with dependency. *Amae* comes from the verb *amaeru*, which Doi defines as "to depend on and to presume on another's love," "to seek and bask in another's indulgence." He believes that the verb *amaeru* is unique to the Japanese language and is not found in other languages, although the phenomenon he describes may be found among other peoples and cultures. As George De Vos notes, *amaeru* designates "passive induction of nurturance towards one's self from others," and such a passive induction "cannot be expressed in an active intransitive verb in Western languages."[25] What happens is that the dependent person consciously or unconsciously manipulates another individual in a dyadic relationship. "To *amaeru*," according to De Vos, "is to produce passively the state of being loved and indulged or appreciated by another, a form of emotional judo."[26]

As may be inferred, *amae* is typical of the behavior of a small child toward its mother. When a child cries and shows other signs of wanting to be picked up by the mother and be cuddled and comforted, a Japanese observer witnessing such a scene would characterize the behavior as a form of *amae*. Doi observes that the desire for *amae* does not disappear as an individual grows up; rather, it continues into adulthood.[27] Such a person, from the more individualistic Western point of view, would probably be characterized as lacking in a fully developed sense of independence and personal autonomy.

The significance of *amae* to Japanese social structure is that the family and small group provide the setting in which an individual can engage in this kind of dependent behavior. For instance, within one's own family, an individual can expect parents and brothers and sisters to overlook whatever shortcomings he or she may have and even to tolerate errant behavior. It is in the nature of things for families to be supportive of their members and to provide understanding and affection. In the Japanese social setting, small groups, like families, are expected to be indulgent toward group members. Nakane, for example, notes that in small groups "the weakness of the superior may be covered by his subordinates, and *vice versa.*"[28] She goes on to say that to "counterbalance the dependence on the leader on the part of his followers, it is always hoped that the leader, in his turn, will be dependent on his men."[29]

Of course, *amae*, or dependency, necessarily implies at least a dyadic relationship. Dependency cannot exist unless there is another person or persons on whom one can be dependent. To put it another way, an individual cannot exist apart from the group. A number of interesting implications follow from this observation.

Doi notes, for example, that in Japanese culture the ideas of private and public are rather poorly developed.[30] One would suppose that this is because privacy has value only to an individual whose goal is self-realization and personal autonomy apart from family and other social groups. If individuals can define themselves only in relation to other people, then privacy cannot be for them a virtue. By extension, the idea of public probably cannot become meaningful without its counterpart, the idea of private. We tend to contrast public and private. The word *public* is an abstraction, and because it is an abstraction, we cannot see it but must infer it. Obviously, it pertains to a collectivity that is greater and broader than the individual, family, or group. Something public exists when human beings who have individual autonomy can have a sense of affinity for other individuals like themselves whom they have never seen or whom they do not know personally, but with whom they share common values and goals. It is instructive that there is no word in the Japanese language for privacy and that the idea of public is expressed by the word *ko*, which means "prince."

Another implication is that, according to Doi, the Japanese have an ambivalent attitude toward the idea of freedom. At one time *jiyu* ("freedom") implied freedom to engage in acts of *amae*, and it was therefore frowned upon as a manifestation of selfishness, egotism, and self-indulgence. As a result of Western influence, the idea of freedom has also become endowed with positive connotations—hence the ambivalence. Doi also argues that in the West the idea of freedom has enabled the individual to assert his independence from the group; in Japan, however, this is impossible—the need for *amae* binds an individual to his group.[31] In other words, a person who is strongly bound to a group because of dependency feelings cannot become free.

In summary, the vertical structure of Japanese society is clearly related to the psychological orientation of the Japanese people. They both work together, so to speak, to keep individuals bound to the group. The group orientation has implications for politics because the social networks in which individuals are enmeshed can serve as mediating variables. We will explore some of these implications in the chapters that follow.

In this regard, Thomas Rohlen's comments are of considerable interest. Rohlen, an anthropologist, studied a Japanese bank. When he looked at its organizational structure, he found support for the concepts proposed by Doi and by Nakane.[32] He found examples "that would affirm the recognition and acceptance of dependency."[33] But he also discovered that the bank's management was ambivalent about dependency. The management tried to discourage dependency of individuals on the organization, that is, on the level of company-individual relations. Yet, at the personal level, dependency remained strong and supported the paternal role of management. Rohlen put it neatly when he remarked, "Independence is not being encouraged when dependency is discouraged; rather the ideal organization man is one who allows others to be dependent on him, but who is not himself dependent on the organization."[34]

Management apparently adopts this stance because the bank's primary goal is profits, which will enable it to grow and to gain a competitive edge over other banks. To be profitable, the bank needs to employ people who are efficient and productive and who are able to show initiative, which means people who are not overly dependent.

When we compare a business organization such as a bank with political parties, some interesting contrasts emerge. If the organizational goal of business firms is to maximize profits, what are the organizational goals of political parties? The answer is not so clear-cut. Is it "aggregating" demands, adopting viable public policies, creating a national consensus on public issues? Even if parties have clear organizational goals, moreover, such goals may very well conflict with the individual goals of party politicians, which is to get elected to office. And one way to get elected is to provide benefits to constituents.

3
A Theory of Japanese Democracy

This chapter will try to pull together the arguments presented in the previous chapters, to elaborate on them where appropriate, and to apply them to the Japanese political system. We began with an outline of the general market model of democracy and suggested a variant of it, an investment model that likens party politicians to entrepreneurs and voters to investors seeking benefits from the political system in return for the investment, which consists of votes and other forms of political support.

In the general market model, benefits occupy a prominent place. Those who use this model tend to stress collective goods or indivisible benefits. Perhaps this is because economics shows how individuals acting out of selfish motives can mutually benefit from entering into economic exchanges; by analogy, political scientists assume that each individual is better off if everyone contributes to the provision of a collective or public good that is available to all than if no one makes the effort. The problem of collective goods, however, is that because they are available to all, individuals are tempted to avoid paying for them, that is, they will try to get a "free ride" by getting others to pay for collective goods. This is one reason why, as Mancur Olson has shown, the coercive power of the state must often be brought into play. As Olson notes, "Despite the force of patriotism, the appeal of the national ideology, the bond of common culture, and the indispensability of the system of law and order, no major state in modern history has been able to support itself through voluntary dues or contributions. . . . Taxes, compulsory payments by definition, are needed."[1]

But, as was suggested earlier, collective benefits are not the only kinds of benefits that ought to be taken into account. There are also divisible benefits that primarily benefit a limited number of citizens, or a localized area, even though these benefits are provided by government authorities using public funds. Public works projects, such as bridge construction, are a typical example. A bridge benefits those who live in the immediate vicinity but not those who live thousands of miles away and never leave home. Where divisible benefits are highly valued, the electoral contest can assume considerable importance. Thus Dennis Mueller writing on public choice notes, "On some issues a voter's benefits from electing one candidate over another may be very high. Tariffs, tax loopholes, a nearby bridge are examples of bills with large benefits for some voters. Thus, the probability of a citizen's voting for a candidate who supports issues promising special, narrow benefits for him may be much greater than for a candidate who supports 'general interest' legislation with equal total benefits for the citizen."[2] Other benefits are patronage, such as those provided by political parties. Finally, there are benefits that accrue to particular individuals.

The kinds of benefits that are sought vary from individual to individual depending on, among other things, the social environment in which the individual is put. The discussion in chapter 2 treated social networks as a significant variable in explaining political behavior, especially electoral choices. If one believes, as I do, that Chie Nakane and Takeo Doi have been reasonably accurate in portraying Japanese society and individual psychology, then it seems reasonable to believe further that social networks represent an important channel for the flow of political information and, more important, political influence. For example, social networks could affect the level of political participation and modify the effect of socioeconomic variables on political behavior. In any case, my working hypothesis is that social networks are much more significant in the Japanese political system than, say, in the American, because in the latter case there is a cultural bias against letting one's political decisions be affected by outside influences. Thus Angus Campbell comments that "voting, whether at the mass or legislative level, is morally a matter of individual judgment and conscience; recognition of group obligation and interests is thoroughly taboo to some Americans."[3]

Other aspects of social networks built on the basis of vertical society are worth stressing. First of all, the basic component of vertical society is the dyad, or a two-person interaction system. One feature of dyads is that they do not suffer from the free rider problem that, according to Olson, characterizes large organizations. Small groups formed on dyadic relationships have a strong incentive to achieve group goals, because it is fairly easy to ascertain which members are not doing their share to promote the good of the group. Moreover, as Luigi Graziano has observed, "In the dyad, the smallest social formation, the incentive is greatest because the dyad does *not* pursue collective goods, but services which are exclusively and immediately meant for the two actors."[4]

A second characteristic of dyads is that there is a direct exchange of favors between the two parties. And, as Graziano suggests, the exchange does not lead to collective goods. This kind of exchange is *direct exchange.*

In contrast to direct exchange, there are forms of *indirect exchange.* Modern society is characterized by a proliferation of complex organizations that require social relationships that go beyond direct exchange between two persons. Complex organizations generally require social relationships that are mediated by social values or goals. That is, people work together because they share common ideals, for example, members of a peace organization.[5] It should be noted that indirect exchange does not necessarily displace direct exchange. The former can often be superimposed on the latter.

There is a third form of exchange, which could be called *generalized exchange* because it involves three or more actors. In generalized exchange, actor A does B a favor, not expecting B to reciprocate but rather anticipating that later C or D or E might return the favor. Generalized exchange "can only operate in an atmosphere of generalized morality and trust that the system will work."[6] According to Peter Ekeh, the conception of citizenship rests on the principle of generalized exchange. An example is a situation where an individual pays taxes and in exchange expects to be protected from illegitimate violence.

Finally, in order to round out the picture, some comments about benefits flowing from exchange transactions should be made. Luigi Graziano has suggested a distinction between *extrinsic* and *intrinsic* benefits. Extrinsic benefits are instrumental benefits, that is, they are tangible gains that originate from social interactions. By contrast, intrinsic benefits are expressive benefits, such as the emotional satisfaction or inspiration individuals get from working for a cause they believe in, from becoming a part of a revolutionary movement, and the like. The reward comes from being associated with the cause or movement, that is, association is an end in itself.[7] The basic assumption of our model is that extrinsic benefits are more important than intrinsic benefits in Japanese politics.

It would be appropriate at this point to return to the investment model. In this model, voters may support politicians in the hope of getting benefits as a return on their investment. No doubt there are persons who invest as individuals on the basis of their calculations of costs and benefits. But there are others who invest as members of a consortium. The consortium is most likely made up of those individuals involved in particular social networks. There are certain advantages to be gained from this kind of an arrangement. First, information costs are reduced for the individual voters since they need only do what others around them are doing. Second, the probability of securing benefits, especially divisible benefits, is enhanced by acting as a group. Politicians are naturally happy when blocs of votes are delivered to them on election day.

Needless to say, different voters and different consortia of voters have different preferences as to the kinds of benefits that are to be made available through political action. It is my belief that much of contemporary Japanese politics can be explained in terms of changing preferences and the ability or inability (or unwillingness) of politicians to respond to the change. I will elaborate on this theme later.

Politics Perceived in Personal Terms

A principal feature of vertical society is that it is based on highly personalized relationships between superiors and inferiors. As explained earlier, these dyadic relationships can serve as building blocks for larger structures that are pyramidal in form. Those who make up the base of the pyramid are linked to the person at the apex through a series of intermediaries. Although the process is a cumbersome one, it is possible in theory and usually in practice for those placed at the lower sections of the pyramidal structure to secure access to those at the upper sections, including the very top. The individual at the bottom appeals to his patron (who happens to be a client of a higher patron) and through him goes up the chain step by step. For example, a farmer might ask his patron, who happens to be the village chief, to help the farmer's son find a suitable position in a government agency. The village chief, in turn, could seek the assistance of his patron, who is a member of the prefectural assembly. The legislator could then ask his patron, a member of the House of Representatives, to use whatever influence he has in getting the young man placed in a government office. As this hypothetical case suggests, individuals relate to the political system essentially through personalized channels. Citizens who can use such personalized channels feel assured that they have access to the political system. Such individuals are likely to have a sense of political competence. They are part of the system and feel that it will respond to their personal needs and demands. In return, of course, these individuals are likely to support helpful legislators in the next election.

Obviously, pyramidal political structures are more likely to be found in rural areas. The situation is rather different in large cities, where the average citizen has almost no opportunity to establish personalized relationships with some local influential or political activist who can put him in touch with higher-level political figures. Such citizens are not able to relate to the political system in a personalized way and hence may feel politically alienated. They do not perceive the system as responsive to them. Their feelings of political competence are likely to be low. (More comments on urban politics will follow.)

Another aspect of personalized politics is that candidates are often more important than issues or party labels. Some voters are willing to vote for candidates recommended by local influentials. Other voters look for the personal qualities of candidates for public office. Among those who seek elective office, the man or woman who has a record of achievement, has acquired a good reputation, and is known to be a person of good character is likely to be favored by the voters. Other things being equal, these personal qualities often carry more weight than a candidate's position on issues and policy matters. In fact, it is quite likely that personal qualities are more important than party affiliation. It may be that many voters eventually develop a commitment to a particular political party by first acquiring the habit of supporting a particular candidate and then adopting the party that the candidate happens to be affiliated with. One of the strengths of the Liberal Democratic party (LDP) is that it has been able to attract candidates who have the qualities that make them appealing to many voters.

Incidentally, legislators who have built up a personalized following can often "bequeath" this political asset to family members, occasionally a widow, but more often to a son or nephew. In the 1976 election, for example, 179 of those elected to the House of Representatives belonged to this category. That is, their fathers, uncles, or some other close kin had been active in politics, either at the local or national level.[8]

The penchant for personalized politics can conceivably be related to the phenomenon of dependency described earlier. Unfortunately, there is apparently no systematic theory about the political consequences of dependency. Robert Lane has argued in his *Political Thinking and Consciousness* that it is necessary for children in all cultures to grow up and assume independent responsibilities and that an individual who has been deprived of independence "is likely to employ political material in these efforts to cope with his deprivation of independence"–to the extent that he is interested in politics. Lane adds that "the political style of those deprived of a sense of independence is likely to be shaped by a search for the authoritative."[9]

Similar views have been expressed by Richard Solomon in his controversial study of Chinese political culture.[10] Speaking of traditional Chinese political culture, he states that most people were nonparticipants in politics, partly because they had been socialized to depend on powerful leaders. "An individual sought security not through his personal efforts, but by adjustment to group norms and interests, and through 'obedient respect' for those with authority."[11] But at the same time, notes Solomon, there was an ambivalent attitude toward political leaders. On the one hand, a strong leader who could maintain control over politics was sought, yet, on the other hand, in their personal relation to the world of politics, many people found it desirable to avoid those in authority because they might be manipulated by powerful leaders.[12]

Regardless of the accuracy of what Lane and Solomon have said about submission to authority, their comments are suggestive for the Japanese case. One would suppose that dependency and authoritarianism would go together. At the same time, it is worth remembering that since 1945 there has been a powerful countervailing force, namely, socialization into democratic norms. The postwar constitution and the institutional reforms sponsored by the occupation are heavily slanted in favor of democracy. In addition, the educational system is an important instrument for inculcating democratic values. Some of the public opinion poll data seem to indicate that in Japan the longer an individual has been exposed to formal schooling, the stronger his preference for democratic values.[13] Finally the mass media, like professional educators, have acquired a vested interest in preventing the reemergence of authoritarian rule, which would put them at a disadvantage. Hence those in the mass media may well see themselves as the guardians of democratic values and processes. Democracy, like good wine, should improve with age, and hence democratic values should become more firmly established as the years go by.

Another important aspect of democracy has to do with political organizations. According to the theory of pluralism, overlapping membership in a variety of organizations representing important economic and other interests in society contributes to the health of a democracy. This is because the electorate, pulled in different directions by conflicting forces as represented in organizations, avoids being split into two mutually antagonistic and irreconcilable groups. Political conflict, according to this theory, is sufficiently restrained by crosscutting memberships to permit an underlying consensus to persist. It follows that political organizations play a vital role in the functioning of a democratic system.

The idea of pluralism, however, has been challenged by Mancur Olson's theory of collective action cited earlier. It will be recalled that, according to Olson, large organizations are likely to fall short of providing an optimal amount of collective good because of the possibilities of members' getting a free ride. Thus, large organizations must depend on "selective benefits" to motivate their leaders. As James Q. Wilson has written, "Pluralists can no longer be confident that organizations will spontaneously emerge to represent any aroused or socially important interest; even more crucial, certain interest classes will be systematically underrepresented owing to their inability to supply either the coercion or the individual inducement sufficient to produce large-scale organization."[14]

Moreover, in the case of Japanese democracy, there is the further problem of conflict between vertical society and the formation of voluntary associations. The importance of vertical ties between patrons and clients tends to impede the development of the horizontal relationships that form the basis of voluntary associations. Thus Nakane notes that "in Japan it is very difficult to form and maintain the sort of voluntary association found so often in Western societies, in that it does not have the basis of frame or existing vertical personal relations."[15] She also notes that there were many attempts after World War II to form voluntary welfare organizations, but that they did not function like their American counterparts "because of lack of organizing personnel, active participation on the part of members and social recognition by the general public."[16]

Political Relevance

One important variable that exerts a powerful influence on what is relevant politically is, oddly enough, an individual's geographical location. This is partly a result of the political system. That is, our elections are based on geographical units, and representatives to the various legislatures—local and national—are elected from electoral districts and presumably represent the economic and other interests of the people who live in that district. In the Japanese case, residence in urban or rural areas makes a difference for fairly obvious reasons.

In Japan, rural hamlets and villages represent a classic case of patron-client systems. In such communities, most of the inhabitants are engaged in agriculture (although recently farmers have also engaged in nonfarming occupations). Moreover, the inhabitants live in close proximity to one another and interact frequently on a face-to-face level. But they also represent more than a mere residence group: their families have probably lived there for a number of generations. In this sense, many persons become members of a rural community through birth rather than through conscious choice; early in life, they are socialized to value group solidarity. All of these factors enhance a sense of identity with the community: what is good for the whole is good for its individual members.

From a political point of view, an important goal is to obtain material resources from outside the community. Japan's modernization and industrialization, at least in its earlier stages, occurred at the expense of the agricultural areas and to the benefit of the cities, which became the centers of economic expansion. Cities, unlike the rural villages, have long provided higher incomes, greater economic opportunities, and a more exciting life. Understandably, the deprived rural dwellers have sought to redress the balance by various measures, including attracting industries and securing funds from the central government to promote public works. Improvements in village facilities—for example, better roads, more schools, and new medical clinics—have obviously helped make life easier for the residents. Since central government funds are often obtained through political means, politics has taken on an instrumental meaning. Political support, especially electoral support, has been exchanged for tangible material benefits to the village or hamlet. Under the circumstances, politics has become very relevant to every resident: he or she stands to gain personally from public works paid for by outside moneys that are brought into the community.

All this, of course, has some interesting implications for political participation. If, following Anthony Downs, one applies a cost-benefit type of analysis, it turns out that the benefits from voting for a candidate who will presumably be helpful in bringing in outside resources can be rather substantial. At the same time, costs are rather low. One does not need to spend a good deal of time collecting information on the various candidates since the local community has already come to a consensus on the most worthy candidate. One needs only to vote with the group. Moreover, voting in this social context is an affirmation of group solidarity. Hence, voting can be something more than a simple political act.

Finally, the Japanese vote is worth more in the rural areas than it is in the cities, which provides an additional incentive to go to the polls on election day. This inequality comes from the apportionment system, which favors the rural constituencies. The present system was laid down in 1947, when the cities were still relatively small because the American bombings of the big cities during the latter stages of World War II had dispersed the urban population. Although the war ended in August 1945, urban residents had not yet returned in full force by 1947. Moreover, since then there has been persistent and large-scale migration into urban areas, particularly around Tokyo and Osaka. Clearly, periodic reapportionment was needed if a reasonable balance was to be maintained between urban and rural election districts. But the ruling party resisted; reapportionment would not have been in its interest, since it is strong in the rural constituencies. In 1967 and again in 1976, reform efforts succeeded in splitting up some of the metropolitan districts, which increased the number of legislators by nineteen in 1967 and twenty in 1976. Despite these efforts, however, urban districts continue to be markedly under-represented. According to an estimate made by the newspaper *Asahi,* the Liberal Democratic party would have obtained twenty-seven fewer seats in the 1976 election if reapportionment based on present population density had been in force.[17]

The value of the vote, together with the other factors enumerated, suggests that political participation, including electoral participation, is likely to be high in rural communities. The situation in the cities, particularly the metropolitan areas, is much more complex. Unlike life in rural hamlets, where the inhabitants know each other personally and interact frequently on a face-to-face basis, life in the cities is ordinarily much more anonymous. Cities contain a significant proportion of people who were not born there but who have moved in to take up residence. Even those who are born in a city are not likely to develop the kind of identification with it that one usually finds in rural hamlets. As a consequence, social interaction on a sustained basis, except among immediate neighbors or relatives, is often rather minimal, with the result that a sense of community is not well developed.

Occupational differentiation in cities, moreover, is much more advanced than in rural areas. Modern industry cannot function without a broad range of workers with specialized skills. At one extreme are corporate executives who manage gigantic corporations, and at the other extreme are unskilled workers who do menial work in shops and factories. Needless to say, there are rather wide variations in income, lifestyle, and political concerns and expectations.

Another important difference between rural and urban areas is that in the latter the residence is often separated from the workplace, whereas in hamlets and villages they may be the same. In urban areas, especially in large metropolitan areas, many gainfully employed people are compelled to commute to their jobs, often long distances. Commuters have sometimes been likened to "boarders": they leave the house early in the morning and do not return until late at night. Because, as has been indicated, urban dwellers generally do not develop a strong sense of attachment to the community, their workplace—factory, plant, store, or office —becomes a kind of substitute for the community. As Nakane puts it, when workplace and residence are not the same, "precedence is given to the place of work, which is their community (the village, as they see it), rather than to the local residential group."[18]

But this presents some problems in a democracy—in which representation is based on geography as determined by the place of residence. What happens if a person lives in one area but is employed in another? The answer appears to be that he or she may not be much interested in what goes on politically in the local community. In many suburban areas, therefore, the more politically active persons are often the housewives and mothers, who stay home with the children while their husbands are at work.

There is, however, one important qualification to this generalization. Labor union membership, for example, can have an effect on an individual's political orientation, although this may not always be the case. In addition to fighting for bread-and-butter issues such as higher wages and better working conditions, Japanese unions tend to adopt ideological goals based, in some instances, on their espousal of Marxist principles; to some extent these goals rub off on their members, but often not to the degree that we might imagine. In patron-client systems, ideology tends to be subordinate to more personal considerations.

There are also marked differences in educational levels between rural and urban areas. The proportion of those with a high school or college education is much higher in the cities. This is obviously related to occupational differentiation. Advanced education enables individuals to qualify to become corporate managers, engineers, computer programmers, and technicians. Education is also an important political variable. Educated people tend to be better informed about politics because they can acquire this information at lower cost, are more critical of the foibles and shortcomings of politicians, and more inclined to be individualistic in their attitudes and behavior, partly because of more exposure to Western democratic norms.

To some degree, the overall variations in political orientation and behavior between rural and urban districts can be attributed to differences in occupation and education (and age—cities have more younger people). For instance, left-wing parties usually get proportionately more votes in the cities, which may be attributed, in part, to the higher proportion of industrialized workers and college-educated people in the cities. But not all of the differences can be attributed to these variables. There is probably a residual difference that stems from the very nature of city life. People who live in cities are forced to interact with strangers; they are exposed to different life-styles and essentially live in a social milieu different from that of rural residents. In other words, city residents present a much more varied picture. And this variety makes urban politics much more fluid, more complicated, and thereby harder to predict.

There is a way, however, to bring some semblance of order into the complex urban picture. First, we would suggest a "dual polity" model of urban politics. According to this model, politics in large urban centers such as Tokyo operates on at least two levels: local and national. At the city ward level, which is the lowest, political patterns seem to be rather similar to those in rural villages. Here one finds local notables—shopkeepers, craftsmen, and professionals—who are active in local politics and give considerable time and attention to it. They operate through neighborhood block associations and other traditional organizations and make their influence felt. Although they may or may not be officially affiliated with the Liberal Democratic party, they are conservative and are in essence supporters of that party. For instance, in 1973, 522 out of 1,047 members of the special ward assemblies in Tokyo were Liberal Democrats. An important difference between the local ward and the rural village is that local, ward-level politics does not appear to be closely linked to national politics through interconnected patron-client clusters, because in national elections held in Tokyo the Liberal Democrats are weaker than they are in rural areas. In other words, patron-client clusters in cities do not necessarily become building blocks for larger systems.

The reason for this discontinuity, one suspects, is that it is difficult to incorporate large numbers of people into personalized social networks that are relevant to politics. For instance, a unionized blue-collar worker who commutes from his apartment in the suburbs to a factory located many miles away is rather different from a farmer who lives in a rural hamlet. In other words, large cities hold countless individuals who are from the political point of view "free-floating," that is, who are not committed to a particular small group that is politically relevant. Such people, therefore, are incorporated, if at all, into the national political system through labor unions, religious organizations such as the Sokagakkai, or support groups established by conservative politicians. Citywide politics represents an intermediate level between national and local politics, and often the personality and qualifications of the candidate are the key factors in achieving victory. If the dual polity model is valid, then one ought not extrapolate from one level to another. This is because city dwellers often differentiate between local and national politics and behave somewhat differently in these areas. (A more detailed discussion will be found in chapter 6.)

Another way to approach urban politics is to sort out city residents by classifying them along two dimensions. The first dimension is their social values, that is, whether they are "traditional" or "modern." By traditional values, we have in mind dependency and preference for diffuse, whole-person relationships, in short, the values that are associated with patron-client systems. Modern values are more universal, individualistic, role-specific values, the kind that are more typical of contemporary Western culture.

The second dimension has to do with the ability or willingness of individuals to work with like-minded people to achieve common objectives, particularly collective goals. Such individuals are seen as "associative," and those who are unable or unwilling to join with others are characterized as "disassociative."

These two models have been derived from models previously proposed by Maruyama Masao and Okuda Michio.[19] I have made modifications and tried to create a composite model based on the work of these two scholars.

The two variables are combined in table 3-1.

Table 3-1

Attitudes, Social Values, and Solidarity

	Traditional	Modern
Associative	1. Dependent	4. Civic-minded
Disassociative	2. Apathetic	3. Privatized

The four categories of attitudes–dependent, apathetic, civic-minded, and privatized—have the following characteristics.

1. Dependency is related to vertical society and is a trait found among individuals who are tradition-oriented and who are part of hierarchically organized social systems. In urban areas such persons are more likely to be found among small shopkeepers and craftsmen, and they may well have been born in a particular district rather than have migrated there from elsewhere.

2. Apathetic individuals have traditional social values but for some reason have not become embedded in locally based social networks. For instance, they may be fairly young recent migrants to the urban areas, have lower levels of education, and do more menial forms of work. In general, people in this category are less attentive to politics, and they have less sense of involvement in city life than do those in the first category.

3. Privatized persons are perhaps better educated than those in the second category. They are also more modern than apathetic individuals, that is, they are more individualistic. Like those in the apathetic category they have a low level of political interest and commitment.

4. Civic-minded people tend to be more individualistic and are willing to form voluntary associations with like-minded people in the pursuit of common goals, particularly those affecting their everyday lives. Kurasawa Susumu's characterization of residents of *danchi* ("large housing projects") in metropolitan areas is relevant here. He describes such people as belonging to the new middle class, as highly educated, relatively young, and engaged in white-collar occupations. They are sensitive to the problems of urban life, aware of their right to enjoy a minimum level of environmental standards, and conscious of the need to engage in collective action to gain their goals. Since they tend

to form a rather homogeneous group sharing common attributes and problems, they can form organizations led by one of their own members who happens to have organizational and negotiating skills. Membership in such organizations is neither automatic nor compulsory but is based on voluntary action on the part of residents. In these organizations, there is a good deal of democratic interaction between the leadership and the rank-and-file. Finally, these organizations are multifunctional but do emphasize instrumental goals, and in their negotiations with government agencies and the housing authority, stress is placed on the attainment of the common interests of the residents.[20]

Our hypothesis is that the "mix" of the four types of attitudes found in urban populations will help explain the kinds of politics, especially electoral politics, that are found in urban districts. To cite an example, in districts where civic-minded individuals are found in large numbers, the probability that citizens' or residents' movements will emerge is higher than in areas where there are many apathetic individuals. Similarly, one would expect considerable support for conservative candidates in districts where the more traditional, dependency-oriented individuals tend to live.[21]

Moreover, it is also our hypothesis that the four categories mentioned above are to some extent related to migration into the big cities. First of all, it should be noted, as James White has shown in his carefully argued essay on cityward migration in Japan, that movement into the metropolitan areas has not resulted in mass alienation and social disorganization, because family, kinship, and informal social ties are not necessarily severed by the migrants.[22] Nevertheless, one would assume that young people who have recently come to the city do not feel fully integrated into the community for some time. Indeed, they may well change jobs and move from one boarding house or apartment to another. For this reason, many of the younger generation probably fall into the apathetic or privatized categories, depending on, among other things, their educational level.

But, as the years go by, these migrants are likely to acquire families and settle down in some part of the city. In so doing, they tend to become incorporated into existing social networks, that is, their level of social integration will rise, and they tend to show more interest in their community and in the kind of social services it can offer to make life more attractive. At some point, then, one would expect that at least some of the migrants will move into the civic-minded category and join the citizens' and residents' associations that have become an established part of the urban scene during the last decade.

It is tempting to assume, as does Okuda for instance, that more and more people, especially in cities, will fall into the civic-minded category, which suggests that eventually Japan will develop a kind of "civic culture."[23] This may happen over the very long run, but probably not in the foreseeable future.

City dwellers are not that much different from their rural counterparts when it comes to seeking improvements in public facilities. They want better roads near their residences, better schools for their children, easy access to clinics and hospitals, and environmental controls to assure a cleaner environment. But many city residents do not perceive a direct relationship between their wants and politics: as has been suggested, their particular social networks may not be part of patron-client clusters that are plugged into the larger networks that provide access to political decision-making structures, as is often the case with rural dwellers. In this sense there is, in urban areas, less awareness of a community held together by personal bonds and common values, interests, and goals; as a result, there is less group pressure to participate in politics, particularly for instrumental goals. An individual who lives in a rural hamlet is aware that he is expected to cast his ballot and that if he does not, his friends and neighbors will surely know about it. By contrast, life in a big city is rather impersonal, and no one much cares whether neighbors have taken the trouble to go to the polls. And, since information costs can be high—city dwellers cannot easily obtain information about candidates from local notables or neighbors—there is less incentive to vote. Finally, in city districts, the ratio of voters to legislative representatives is higher than in rural districts, which means that the value of each urban vote is correspondingly lower. All in all, one expects the level of political participation in cities, particularly in metropolitan areas, to be lower than in the rural districts.

Political Cleavages

Almost everywhere political action intended to achieve the collective good is hampered by the existence of barriers that divide populations into indifferent or hostile camps. Some nations find themselves torn by religious controversies, others by ethnic or racial conflicts. In some countries, language becomes a focal point of contention, as for example between the English-speaking and French-speaking peoples in Canada. In other nations, regional divisions greatly strain the political fabric—e.g., cities against the rural areas, the industrialized regions against the farming districts.

Fortunately for contemporary Japan, none of the factors that cause serious political divisions is present. But, as is true with all advanced industrial societies organized on capitalistic principles, conflict, either actual or potential, that flows from inequalities in wealth, income, social status and prestige, does exist. In other words, socio-economic status is a significant source of political cleavage.

An industrial society is by its very nature highly differentiated: that is, it requires division of labor and specialization. Moreover, the range of specialized occupations is wide and getting wider every day. To get these jobs, people need more education and training, and those who have training that is in demand can command higher wages. Thus wide variations develop among the population as to the kind of work people do, the amount of education they have, and the incomes they receive. These variations often lead to differences in life-styles. As a result, individuals with similar backgrounds and life-styles tend to associate with one another and to become cut off socially from those who belong to other classes. When this happens, many begin to perceive society as being structured along class lines.

An awareness that society is divided into classes is not important politically so long as people accept such divisions as a "natural" condition of the social order. If there is a broad consensus regarding the class system, political problems are not likely to arise. The picture changes, however, if some groups seek to improve their economic position by political means. For example, the emergence of a political party (or parties) that openly and explicitly claims to represent the economic interests of a single class will have the effect of polarizing politics for other parties, which would have either to espouse the interests of other classes or to deny the validity of class-based parties. In any case, a democratic system whose viability depends on the existence of an underlying consensus of values would find itself under strain. In contemporary Japan, all of the opposition parties —Socialist, Democratic Socialist, Clean Government, and Communist (but not the New Liberal Club)—advocate some form of "socialism." The Democratic Socialists are the most moderate and see themselves as a national party, but the Socialist and Communist parties accept to varying degrees the fundamental premises of Marxist theory regarding the conflictual role of classes in politics.

Despite the existence of self-proclaimed class parties, however, the attractiveness of class appeals is bound to be attenuated in Japan, given its cultural values and social structure. For instance, *wa*, or social harmony, has traditionally occupied a dominant place in Japanese cultural values. Moreover, vertical society seems to encourage interclass interaction and ties, which has the effect of reducing feelings of class hostility. Nakane's views on this point are instructive: "Even if social classes like those in Europe can be detected in Japan, and even if something vaguely resembling those classes that are illustrated in the textbooks of Western sociology can also be found in Japan, the point is that in actual society this stratification is unlikely to function and that it does not really reflect the social structure."[24]

Another factor, namely, social mobility, also influences class consciousness. Martin Lipset and Reinhard Bendix have put forward the hypothesis (on the basis of American and European experience) that interclass mobility tends to weaken working-class solidarity. They argue that those who rise to middle-class status become conservative and that those who are reduced to working-class status retain their conservatism. "Thus, the process of social interchange through which some men rise in status and others fall weakens the solidarity and the political strength of the working class."[25] The role of social class in Japanese politics will be discussed in chapter 4. Suffice it to say here that the data suggest that identification with the middle sectors of society is increasing

We would expect, then, that the relationship between class and party in Japan is rather tenuous. Although some parties openly court the working-class vote, not all workers support such parties. By the same token, not all middle-class voters back the conservative Liberal Democratic party.

If, as we have suggested, social differentiation along class lines does not appear to be very clearly reflected in political cleavages, we may then ask if other factors provide the basis for cleavages. To find the answer, we must go back to the idea of vertical society, psychological dependency, and the cultural factors that go with them.

Our underlying assumption is that Japanese values,

institutions, and social processes tend to support personalized hierarchical relationships and that the political party
that most clearly articulates these is the conservative Liberal
Democratic party. One might even say that Japanese social
traditions are crystallized in this party. The normal expectation is that individuals, whatever their social class and
economic condition, would support this party. But obviously not everyone does, and those who do not may therefore be
looked upon as representing some sort of deviation.

Our first hypothesis is that one important source of this
deviation is Western culture, with its bias in favor of
individualism and democratic institutions. Particularly
since 1945, the Japanese have been subjected, both willingly
and unwillingly, to the onslaught of Western cultural
influences.

Our second hypothesis is that what Nakane has called
"frame" is closely related to the question of political cleavages. Nakane's frame is described as follows: "Frame may
be a locality, an institution or a particular relationship
which binds a set of individuals into one group: in all cases
it indicates a criterion which sets a boundary and gives a
common basis to a set of individuals who are located or
involved in it."[26]

The above definition specifies a locality, institution, or
particular relationship. A prime example of a locality is a
rural village where the inhabitants know each other well and
interact frequently. But not all Japanese live in rural
settings. They increasingly live in towns and cities, where
life is necessarily more anonymous and impersonal than in
rural communities. In this case, the place where one works—
a factory, store, or office—takes the place of a locality.[27] This
is an example of a "particular relationship." Finally, a
school or university is a typical instance of an institution.

The frame is important because those individuals who are
"bound" by it are under some pressure to conform to group
norms. When the frame involves few people, a relatively

high degree of conformity might be expected. It is a characteristic of small groups that members interact frequently, and according to George Homans, "The more frequently persons interact with one another, the more alike in some respects both their activities and sentiments tend to become."[28] In addition, it is more likely that in such a frame the leader or patron is able to guide the group better than in diffuse groups. Take, for example, a small, family-operated business enterprise. Its employees, who are relatively few in number, are likely to be strongly influenced by the owner, and the inference is that their political preferences tend to conform to those of their employer.

To put it in more general terms, those who take patron roles (for example, owners of businesses and those in management positions) are likely to favor the Liberal Democrats; and, in relatively small and cohesive frames, where the element of paternalism is strong, the political attitudes and (more important) the behavior of group members are likely to be close to those of their patrons. In short, we expect paternalism to be positively correlated with Liberal Democratic leanings.

But a complex industrial society needs and develops large-scale organizations and institutions. Obviously, Japan has large, highly capitalized corporations, complex governmental bureaucracies, huge labor union federations with millions of members, and so on. Nevertheless, the core of these large organizations and institutions is still made up of small, patron-client clusters. But at the same time, the frame that encompasses such small groups can be rather large, which means, among other things, that the element of paternalism is weakened. For understanding Japanese politics, two large organizations or institutions are worth special attention, namely, labor unions and colleges and universities.

Neither unions nor institutions of higher learning are indigenous to Japan. Both were imported from the West.

The first unions were formed around the turn of the century by a small group of intellectuals who had learned about socialism from Europe and America and became interested in introducing it into their own country. Thus the labor movement and socialism were joined from the beginning, and it is instructive that the connection still remains, almost three-quarters of a century later. If appears that large organizations often retain for a very long time the characteristics they acquired when they were founded.

The universities were established somewhat earlier than the unions. The government was a prime mover, and one of the purposes was to train future bureaucrats and other members of the elite. Both the universities, and to a lesser extent the unions, were strongly influenced by Western models. Indeed, the universities have become one of the most important transmission belts for the diffusion of Western culture, the other being the mass media.

Given their origins, then, it is perhaps not surprising that unions and universities represent a source of deviation. Both challenge some of the basic assumptions and values of traditional Japanese culture by espousing foreign-derived countermyths such as Marxism and liberal democracy. Thus, both unions and universities may be looked upon as representing deviant subcultures. Those who are placed in this subculture—unionized workers, university faculty and students—frequently do not conform politically to the dominant Japanese institutions and cultural norms; that is, they are more likely to be radical than conservative.

What about those for whom there is no politically relevant frame, for instance, artists, writers, and professionals such as doctors and musicians? In these instances, it is more difficult to predict whether they will conform to the dominant cultural values. One important variable here is probably the degree to which such individuals feel the need to assert their own ideas and tastes. Those who feel the need to be nonconformist very likely reject to some degree the traditional culture and, to the extent that such rejection takes political form, support reformist parties. Many writers and artists, for example, probably fall into this category.

The frame, then, may be seen as mediating between class and party. That is, the frame can sometimes have a powerful effect on the way an individual votes, and the way the electorate divides on election day ultimately determines which group of political leaders will govern the nation.

To the extent that the frame serves as a mediating variable, it can modify the power of the standard demographic variables, such as education, occupation, social class, and place of residence, to predict political behavior. That is, it is often assumed that the standard demographic factors are correlated in a general way with individual political attitudes (by way of socialization processes), so that demographic variables can often serve as surrogate measures of preferences for different kinds of public policies. For instance, it is often assumed that those who belong to the upper classes prefer the status quo and that those in the lower classes prefer political change, usually in a radical direction. In this case, then, social class can be used to predict support for political parties, the upper-class voters backing the conservatives, and the lower-class voters backing the radical party or parties. But if frame serves as a mediating variable, it can modify the relationship predicted, so that individuals who belong to the working class may well vote for the conservative party.

Factionalism and Leadership

So far the discussion of political cleavages has mostly concerned horizontal divisions. But a vertical society also suffers from another kind of cleavage, namely, vertical fissures. We are familiar with them under the name of factionalism.

Vertical society seems to provide a favorable environment for the growth of factions. The appearance of factions seems to be related to two factors. First, since in patron-client systems personal ties assume importance, there is a practical limit to the size of pyramids based on such ties. After all, each individual can interact on a personal basis with only a limited number of individuals. Second, these pyramids generally culminate in one leader at the top. One of the functions of a leader is to provide resources for his followers and subfollowers. And here again there is a limit to the amount of resources any one person is able to muster. Hence patron-client systems also affect the nature of leadership.

A leader cannot exist alone; by definition, a leader needs followers. The study of leadership, therefore, involves the study of group processes. Because of the overwhelming importance of small groups in Japanese society, the discussion of leadership will focus particularly on leadership within small groups.

As Nakane has shown, an important principle that underlies the structure of dyadic groups in Japan is seniority.[29] Groups have a hierarchical structure that is characterized by a delicate and intricate ranking system. Once established, the rank order does not change, and newcomers must necessarily enter at the bottom. Only those who have been in a group or organization for a long time and have worked up from below can hope to become a leader. Alternatively, an ambitious individual who seeks leadership status can, if blessed with sufficient resources, acquire followers and thereby become a leader. In any case, the seniority principle operates in such a way that someone cannot be brought in from outside of the group and function effectively as a leader. This often presents serious problems connected with succession.

Second, a group leader needs to have good working relations with the outside environment. This is probably true of groups everywhere and is not particularly characteristic of Japanese groups. Sidney Verba has noted that "many studies of on-going groups and organizations have found that the group leader is more active in contacts with the external environment of the group than are the other group members."[30] An important job of political leaders in Japan is to bring in resources from the outside to sustain the group.

Third, as students of small group processes have discovered, there are two aspects to leadership: instrumental and affective. One function of a leader is to set the goals of the group and direct its members toward the achievement of such goals. This is the instrumental function. The leader comes up with new ideas, makes suggestions, gives orders. But at the same time the leader must also satisfy the need for affect. A good leader is one who pays attention to the emotional needs of the followers and enhances friendly and harmonious feelings among group members.[31] Because strong dependency feelings are a part of the Japanese personality structure, it would appear that the affective function of leadership is particularly important in the Japanese social context. A good leader must be paternalistic, that is, involved in the emotional and personal life of his followers. The leader also carries the heavy burden of responsibility. "Japanese paternalism," states George De Vos, "still derives much of its strength from the traditional expectation that a person playing the role of a boss (literally, in Japanese, *oyabun*, "parent role") will assume almost total responsibility for the health and welfare of his workers. The belief that one's boss has a strong feeling of responsibility allows subordinates the complementary expressive feelings of dependency and loyalty toward authority."[32]

The instrumental and affective functions of leadership tend to work at cross-purposes. That is, the more a leader directs the members of the group, the lower the affective level within the group. Verba believes that "the individual who attempts to control the instrumental activities of the group lowers his chances to be highly thought of by the group according to an affective criterion."[33] One way to avoid this conflict between the instrumental and affective aspects of leadership is for the group leader to give the impression that he is acting not as an individual but in response to some impersonal force, such as "the demands of the situation" or group norms. According to Verba, "The invocation of some external authority by the group leader relieves the follower of the burden of accepting the control of another individual."[34]

This may be true in American society, which prizes autonomy in individuals and therefore stresses externally derived norms and rules to govern interpersonal behavior. But there is considerable evidence that in Japanese society formal rules carry little force in interpersonal relationships such as those found in small groups. A more plausible hypothesis is that the conflict between instrumental and affective functions is minimized if the leader does not exercise the instrumental function directly. Studies of group decision making in Japan have shown that the leader does not give orders, but rather that the subordinates lay their ideas before the superiors and have them adopted. Proposals often originate somewhere within the group, and after prolonged discussion a group consensus emerges. When that happens, the leader does not have to persuade the rank-and-file to accept the decision, since they have already participated in the decision-making process. Quite clearly this process helps to keep affective levels high, but it seems likely that there is a price to be paid for such gains. The price is that creative leadership may well be inhibited. Can this kind of decision making produce leaders who are capable of taking innovative action when confronted by new situations?

Finally, the stress placed on the affective side of leadership affects popular attitudes toward political leaders, especially at the national level. As Verba has rightly pointed out, leadership in small groups is something different from leadership in the political arena. In small group situations, the "no conflict" assumption may be justified. That is, there may be a "single group goal or single method of attaining a group goal that is in the best interests of all concerned—both leaders and followers."[35] In most political situations, however, conflict is inevitable: no matter what policy is adopted, somebody or some group will be hurt. When this happens, the national leader who is identified with that policy is likely to be the target of strong criticism for failing to be "impartial."

Moreover, given the vertical society and the strong sense of dependency that goes with it, political leaders who are outside of one's frame are likely to be regarded with some sense of distrust. They tend to be seen as "outsiders." Hence they are not likely to be the object of affection. Analysts have often commented on the low regard the Japanese public has toward political leaders at the national level. Thus, despite feelings of dependency, many among the mass public are not happy about turning over the reins of government to their leaders: they simply to not trust their national leaders.

Finally, there is no way a politician can personally look after and meet the emotional needs of hundreds of thousands or even millions of people. He cannot possibly treat everyone as he treats his followers, that is, his lieutenants. It probably can be said as a general proposition that the larger the group, the lower the affect level. For instance, if a leader has three followers, he can interact with all of them frequently and be personally involved with their welfare in an intimate way. The result would be a high level of affect. If the group is enlarged to fifty, the leader cannot interact as frequently with all of the followers, and so the affect level should be somewhat lower. It is instructive, in this connection, that Japanese prime ministers are seldom looked upon with affection or enjoy widespread popular support.

Some Implications for Public Policy

Downs suggests that party politicians seek political office to obtain "income, prestige, and power," rather than to carry out particular public policies. "They treat policies purely as means to the attainment of their private ends, which they can reach only by being elected."[36] The "name of the game" for individual politicians, according to this view, is to win in every election.

But politics is necessarily a group enterprise. A solitary politician working by himself has little power. Politicians must organize themselves into political parties, which Downs defines as "a coalition of men seeking to control the governing apparatus by legal means."[37] Control of the governing apparatus brings tremendous advantages to the coalition: power, prestige, and above all access to the tremendous financial resources that the state controls through its power to tax and disperse funds. As is well known, conservative politicians have controlled the governing apparatus in Japan most of the time since 1945. Since its formation in 1955, the Liberal Democratic party has been the ruling coalition.

The Liberal Democratic party has maintained itself by successfully mobilizing a substantial bloc of voters, particularly those residing in the rural areas. It has rewarded its faithful followers by providing them with material benefits in the way of grants and subsidies to farmers and agricultural communities and psychic benefits in the way of enhanced feelings of access to the political system, that is, more political competence.

By being assured of continued political support, the Liberal Democratic party elite has been freed to pursue national policies that promote economic growth in general and corporate business in particular. In foreign relations, it has been able to follow a pro-American foreign policy, which has been instrumental in giving Japanese business access to the huge American market and in keeping national defense costs at an abnormally low level, thanks to the U.S. nuclear umbrella.

Ironically, as will be discussed in detail in chapter 5, economic prosperity and growth have not rebounded to the advantage of the ruling party, which has seen its electoral strength slowly but surely decline. Part of the reason is that

opposition forces have been able to mount a counter-
mobilization by appealing to individuals and groups that,
for one reason or another, find Liberal Democratic control
distasteful. But so far the opposition forces have not
succeeded in gaining "control of the governing apparatus,"
partly because they have not been able to unite (owing to
ideological differences and organizational difficulties) and
partly because the present electoral system works against
them. Figure 3-1 shows the relationship between votes for
the Liberal Democratic party and the party's seats in the
House of Representatives. The scatterplot shows that between 1958 and 1976 both the votes won by Liberal Democratic candidates for the House of Representatives and the
percentage of seats declined. The decline in seats, however,
was not so severe as the loss in votes. Every time the ruling
party lost 1 percent of the vote, it lost roughly 0.7 percent of
the seats in the House of Representatives. As a result,
although the ruling party has not enjoyed the support of the
majority of the electorate since 1967, it has continued to hold
monopoly control of the government by virtue of capturing
more than half of the seats. The December 1976 election for
the House of Representatives proved, however, to be something of a turning point: for the first time, the ruling party
failed to secure a majority in the lower house. The final tally
showed that the Liberal Democratic party had won 249 (48.7
percent) of 511 seats on the basis of 23.65 million votes (41.8
percent of the total votes cast). The ruling party went into the
election in the midst of the Lockheed scandal, in which a
number of conservative politicians, including Tanaka
Kakuei, a powerful faction leader and former prime minister, were accused of having accepted bribes from the Lockheed Corporation. (See chapter 7 for more details.)

A related development that also adversely affected the
ruling party was the resignation from the party of five young
politicians who subsequently formed a splinter group that
called itself the "New Liberal Club." The splinter group

did much better than expected, obtaining seventeen seats and a little more than 4 percent of the popular vote.

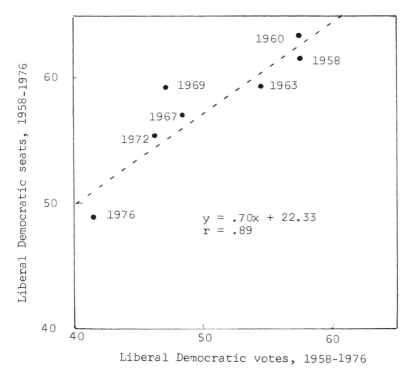

Figure 3-1. Relationship Between Votes and Seats in the House of Representatives for the Liberal Democratic Party, 1958-1976. Note: This is an example of linear regression, a technique that relates 2 variables, x (independent) and y (dependent). The x variable is plotted along the horizontal and and the y variable along the vertical axis. R shows the relationship along a 1 to 0 scale, with 1 showing a perfect relationship. The equation is the mathematical representation of the best fitting line.

Despite their initial defeat, the Liberal Democrats were able to salvage the situation by persuading eight politicians who had been elected as independents to join the party, and by this maneuver, the party was able to secure 257 seats, which was barely sufficient to command a majority, thus enabling it to form a government without having to take in coalition partners from one or more of the opposition parties.

Sooner or later, however, some kind of coalition arrangement will become necessary. That the party that had failed to get the support of more than 50 percent of the electorate could continue to monopolize power was due, of course, to the electoral system, which worked in its favor, a situation that contravenes one of the basic tenets of democratic theory, the rule of the majority. Of course, even if the ruling party actually represented the majority of voters, it is difficult to see how such a majority could consistently rule, given the fragmentation that appears to be inherent in vertical society. For one thing, the prospects of a majority's forming around any vital public issue are not all that encouraging, and even if such a majority position should emerge, the probability of translating the majority view into public policy is not high. This is not surprising. Robert Dahl, in looking at American democracy, has suggested that "on matters of specific policy the majority rarely rules."[38]

The logical implication of all this is that minorities actually govern. "Elections and political competition," says Dahl, "do not make up for government by majorities in any significant way, but they vastly increase the size, number, and variety of minorities whose preferences must be taken into account by leaders in making policy choices."[39] In Japan, minorities within the Liberal Democratic party structure, or those closely associated with the party, find themselves in a favored position, especially when it comes to sharing in the distribution of resources. Other minorities are not likely to do so well, and some may have to be content with exercising veto power. This is the case, for example, with labor unions, which do not have access to the Liberal

Democratic party leaders because of union support for the opposition parties. Unions, however, can prevent the ruling party from enacting blatantly antilabor legislation.

But in the longer view, government ought to involve more than the appeasement of minorities. After all, there is something called the "general welfare." As noted earlier, Mancur Olson has demonstrated that in large organizations the optimum amount of collective good is not likely to be achieved. This should be even more true in a patron-client democracy, which develops powerful pressures to satisfy the particular needs of client-followers at the expense of the larger public interest.

One of the consequences of the relative inability of the political system to promote the general welfare is political apathy and even alienation. Perhaps because of the personalized nature of politics, alienation appears to be directed more at the political leaders than at the system itself. Moreover, it takes the form of distrust of politicians.[40] Our view is that the erosion of trust began with the educated classes and spread to the rest of the population through the educational system and the mass media. One clue may be found in the responses to the national character surveys carried out by the Institute of Mathematical Statistics (Tokeisuri Kenkyujo) between 1953 and 1968. In four surveys undertaken at five-year intervals, the institute asked respondents the following question: "Some people say that if we get good political leaders, the best way to improve the country is for the people to leave everything up to them, rather than for the people to discuss things among themselves." Table 3-2 gives the responses of those who disagree with the statement. The Institute of Mathematical Statistics has interpreted the responses as a measure of opposition to authoritarianism. It suggests the diffusion of democratic norms. But cannot the responses also be interpreted as an indication of the growing distrust of political leaders? If

people trusted the leaders, they would be more willing to let
them govern the country.

Table 3-2

Disagreement with Statement that "Everything
Should be Left Up to Political Leaders,"
1953-1968

Year	National sample	College graduates	Difference
1953	38%	62%	24%
1958	44	63	19
1963	47	58	11
1968	51	65	14

Source: Tokeisuri Kenkyujo. Dai-2 Nihonjin no
         Kokuminsei (Japanese National Character,
         Volume 2). Tokyo, 1970, p. 474.

In any case, one suspects that the reluctance to turn
government over to the politicians, which is most pronounced among the educated sectors of the general population, is related to the influence of Western values and ideals.
There is a tendency, especially among those with higher
education, to compare political reality in Japan with a
highly idealized version of Western democracy. Seen against
such an idealized standard, Japanese democracy, whose
performance tends to fall short of promoting the general
welfare at a high level, evokes a critical response among
those who make the comparison.

However, government is more than the activities of
politicians. There is another institution, one that is insu-
lated to a considerable degree from electoral politics, namely, the bureaucracy. Civil servants are recruited on the basis
of merit as evidenced by the ability to pass competitive exam-

inations. Thus their right to secure a job and retain it are not dependent on "bribing the voters," as some would put it. In this sense, they enjoy a good deal of autonomy and are subject to less pressure than elective officials, who are wont to trade favors for votes.

Moreover, the Japanese bureaucracy from its inception in the latter part of the nineteenth century has resisted demands from political party leaders that government service be opened up to the spoils system. In addition, the bureaucracy has a long tradition of taking the leadership in developing the country into a modern industrial power. J. P. Nettl has argued that Japan represents "the first historical example of a developing nationalism, a value system for which the bureacracy helped to mobilize commitment."[41] Nettl makes the further observation that, in general, bureaucracies "are themselves institutional interest groups with their own interest and goals to defend"[42]—a characterization that would appear to apply to the Japanese case. Furthermore, he sees evidence in Japan of "inter-bureaucratic competition for social goal-setting."[43] Thus, the bureaucracy enjoys considerable autonomy and is to that extent removed from the workings of the party system with its pork-barrel proclivities. If there is any one institution that looks upon itself as the guardian of the general interest, it is the bureaucracy.

One would assume that what sustains the bureaucracy is an underlying consensus regarding its proper role. An obvious weakness of a highly personalized political system is favoritism and nepotism, where individuals are allocated positions on the basis of personal considerations rather than on merit and ability. Favoritism and corruption have a markedly baneful effect on bureaucratic performance, to the detriment of the national interest. It is interesting to note that the same policy of recruitment by means of competitive examinations is also used in the admission of students to most universities and in hiring procedures in many large business firms. It appears that the Japanese are committed to performance and that they are consciously or unconsciously trying to compensate for weaknesses inherent in their social and political system.[44]

The existence of a reasonably autonomous bureaucracy chosen on the basis of merit is also significant because it serves as a kind of "frame" for the political structure. Nakane puts it this way:

> Competing clusters, in view of the difficulty of reaching agreement or consensus between clusters, have a diminished authority in dealings with the state administration. Competition and hostile relations between the civil powers facilitate the acceptance of state power and, in that [the] group is organized vertically, once the state's administrative authority is accepted, it can be transmitted without obstruction down the vertical line of the group's internal organization. In this way, the administrative web is woven more thoroughly into Japanese society than perhaps any other in the world.[45]

In this view, it is the bureaucratic structure that gives society a sense of coordination and enables it to work toward its goals.

Our account of the bureaucracy to this point has revolved around its autonomy, but for the sake of accuracy, the argument should not be carried too far. Although the various ministries and agencies originate a large number of the legislative proposals, the assent of the ruling party, especially its leaders, is required before a bill can become law. Obviously, it is hard to ascertain how often and how much the bureaucrats tailor the bills to the anticipated responses of the party leadership, but one has to suppose that this does occur. Bureaucrats, like everyone else, do not like to engage in futile exercises. We would assume that the bureaucracy and the ruling party try to reach some sort of accommodation on legislative and other programs.

Two factors may facilitate this accommodation. The first is the practice whereby bureaucrats upon retirement run for office with the endorsement of the Liberal Democratic party. Since the credentials of ex-bureaucrats tend to impress many voters, some of these ex-bureaucrats will win electoral contests; once elected, they rise to leadership positions by virtue of their expertise in administration and their connections with bureaucrats still in office. The second factor, which is related to the first, is that some civil servants contemplating entering elective politics upon retirement will begin to cultivate friendships and even support among the clients of the agency where they are employed. In this way they build up a following that can be used later to mobilize voters.

Concluding Remarks

This chapter began with a discussion of the investment model of democracy, and it would be appropriate to return to it. Investors are basically interested in returns, or benefits. Traditionally, much of Japanese politics has involved the pursuit of divisible benefits, such as public works projects and favors for special interests. The demand for divisible benefits has been particularly strong in rural areas, where voters organized into consortia are in a position to provide solid support for the ruling Liberal Democratic party.

But in recent years, the cities have grown tremendously, and with that growth have come new problems. The more traditional highly personalized style of politics is no longer quite appropriate in urban areas, but the ruling party has not been able to respond sufficiently to the changes that have occurred. This is partly because the electoral system is biased against urban areas, resulting in their underrepresentation within the ruling party. As a result, urban voters seeking indivisible benefits have turned away from the Liberal Democratic party or have dropped out of the political process. We will explore these developments in more detail in the following chapters.

Part 2
Empirical Studies

4
Class, Party, and Social Networks

In a democracy, class and party are necessarily related. Social class influences the distribution and allocation of things that are valued in society—income, prestige, deference, power—and therefore acts as the source of cleavages and conflicts. Parties, by contrast, are interested in securing control of the government. In order to do so, they must seek to maximize the support they get from the electorate by stressing consensus. If parties existed completely apart from social classes, they would most likely lead an ephemeral existence. They would come and go and lack the ability to sustain themselves over an extended period of time. At the other extreme, if parties mirrored faithfully all social cleavages and conflicts, they would be unable to achieve the minimum sense of consensus necessary to carry on government in a meaningful way. Thus parties need to have a social basis, but at the same time they must function in such a way as to ameliorate class conflict. Finally, in some instances, class conflict can be dampened by the existence of social networks that promote interaction between superiors and inferiors.

Alternative Models

Two models may be used to help analyze the effects of social class on political parties in developed nations. The first is the "middle majority" model, which postulates an expansion in the number of individuals who occupy the middle sectors of society. Specifically, this model assumes that the upper-working class and middle classes will increase relative to the entire population and eventually come to outnumber those in the upper-middle and lower-working classes.[1] This trend, of course, is attributed to the high economic growth and affluence that has characterized the advanced industrial nations in recent decades. As incomes have risen, economic differentials between classes have declined, and the life-styles of middle-class and working-class people have tended to merge. The political consequence of these changes, it is argued, is a decline in class conflict based on sharp ideological differences. As Morris Janowitz and David Segal have put it, "The politics of the 'middle majority' implies, of course, not the end of party divisions, but a narrowing of party differences and a transformation in the political consequences of these divisions."[2]

The alternative and more plausible model is the "consensus and cleavage" model. It is more complex than the "middle majority" model but, like the latter, assumes that cleavages and conflicts stemming from the social stratification system are reflected in politics. It does not conclude, however, that affluence will do away with political extremism and confrontation politics based on sharp ideological differences. Rather, it assumes that with social and political change, other sources of conflict can emerge. Moreover, it holds that other factors, for instance, ethnicity, race, religion, sex, and age, can also lead to social conflict.

At the same time, according to this model, certain forces and trends lead to consensus. For instance, political parties manage to win the allegiance of individuals from different social classes, and institutions and structures—voluntary associations, for example—help to bring about political integration. Thus, Heinz Eulau, looking at the American political system with its pluralistic democracy and two-party system, has suggested that there is a moving equilibrium in America between cleavage and consensus. He notes that "the fact that party roles can be taken independently of class suggests that the propensity for cleavage due to restrictions imposed by the class system is offset by consensual tendencies arising out of the party system and cutting across class lines."[3]

What is the situation in the Japanese political system?

Social Stratification in Japan

It is not easy to characterize the social stratification system in contemporary Japan. Depending on what criteria are used, different observers draw somewhat different profiles of the social class system. With regard to an industrial society, however, most would agree that occupation is a critical variable because it affects income and social prestige and that five broad occupational categories may be distinguished: professional and managerial, self-employed (in nonagricultural pursuits), white-collar, blue-collar, and farmers and fishermen. There also appears to be a consensus that of these five classes, the professional and managerial ought to be placed at the top. On the basis of income the self-employed category would probably come next. Farmers are sometimes included among the self-employed and sometimes treated separately. White-collar workers would rank higher than blue-collar workers because they are generally paid more. Thus the ranking system suggested by Naoi Atsushi appears to be reasonable (table 4-1).

Several things should be noted about the Japanese social stratification system. The proportion of individuals who are self-employed (including farmers) is rather high: 33 percent. This figure appears to include family members who help on family farms and who work in family-owned and

Table 4-1

Social Class Ranking by
Percentage of Population

Elite (professional and managerial)	10%
Self-employed (in nonagricultural pursuits)	16
White collar	22
Blue collar (nonagricultural)	34
Farmers	17

Source: Naoi Atsushi et al. Hendoki no Nihon Shakai (Japanese Society in a Period of Change). Tokyo, 1972, p. 93.

Note: Total is less than 100% because of rounding.

family-operated stores, shops, and offices. Thus, the white-collar and blue-collar categories are larger than suggested below.

Over the years the proportion of self-employed individuals has tended to decline, but even though some drop out because of retirement, business failures, and the like, this group also recruits new members. In recent years, there has apparently been an increase in the number of young college graduates who, after working for a time in a large firm or factory, try to set themselves up as independent businessmen.

In 1970 the total work force came to about 52 million out of a population of a little more than 100 million. An additional 18 to 20 million adults (twenty years of age or over) were not employed, many of them housewives. It is, of course, the adult population that is important from the political point of view. About 8 to 9 percent of the work force is under twenty years of age, and since the voting age is twenty, this part of the work force cannot participate in politics, that is, in elections. Not all union members, therefore, can be mobilized to vote for leftist parties. For instance, many assembly line workers in electronics plants are girls who have recently graduated from junior high schools. It is hard to believe that girls of this age are highly motivated to participate actively in politics.

Another way to look at social stratification is in terms of upper, middle, and lower. The middle majority model assumes continued expansion of the middle sector. When Japanese respondents are asked to place themselves in one of these three classes, most of them are able to do so. The empirical data suggest that with the passage of years the proportion of those who place themselves in the middle has increased. This can be seen in table 4-2. In 1955, 42 percent placed themselves in the middle sector, but by 1972 the percentage had risen to 73 percent, an increase that is understandable, given the consistently high economic growth rate that Japan achieved during the 1960s. The middle majority model would appear to be applicable to some extent in Japan in recent years.

Table 4-2

Changes in Class Identification, 1955-1972

Year	Upper	Upper middle	Lower middle	Upper lower	Lower lower	Not clear
1955	0	7%	35%	38%	10%	2%
1965	0	12	42	32	9	4
1972	3	35	38	12	4	8

Source: Naoi, <u>Hendoki no Nihon Shakai</u>, p. 98.

Class and Party

Our next step is to examine the relationship between political party preference and social class. How much of an impact does class have on politics?

In an essay written in the mid-1960s, which has attracted considerable attention, Watanuki Joji suggested that cleavages in Japanese society reflect differences in "value systems" more than "economic or status differences."[4] He arrived at this conclusion by examining survey data that showed no clear-cut relationship between income levels and party choice. He found that there were a number of "Tory" workers, that is, manual workers who did not support the leftist parties which explicitly sought labor backing. He also discovered that those who belonged to the white-collar group showed a rather high rate of support for leftist parties. He did not completely dismiss the economic factor, saying, "This is not to deny the working of economic or status interests in Japanese politics," but he did feel that "cultural" or "value" factors were more dominant and that they were superimposed on the economic.[5] Although he does not explicitly state his position, he seems to be siding with those who have adopted the "consensus and cleavage" model.

Although Watanuki's characterization of the relationship between class and party is correct, his argument that "cultural" and "value" factors account for cleavages in Japanese society leaves something to be desired. To begin with, culture is such a broad category that almost anything can be explained by it. Virtually the same thing can be said of value. Undoubtedly, cultural and value factors are at work, but one needs to be more specific, above all to state the relationship of one or more cultural variables to some other variable. It is true that Watanuki does attempt this in some cases. For instance, he explains the support that individuals in the lower strata in both the rural and urban areas give to the conservatives, i.e., the Liberal Democrats, by relating it to village solidarity and hierarchical interpersonal relationships, both of which are buttressed by traditional values. The leftist inclinations of the white-collar class are accounted for in Watanuki's essay by several factors: "This phenomenon is not caused by any single factor, but it is the result of the coincidence of many."[6] Among them are age, membership in unions, and antagonism to traditional values.

In attempting to sort out the several variables that account for political cleavages, it is perhaps best to begin with responses to traditional values. As has been suggested in earlier chapters, vertical society and dependency are related, two sides of the same coin, as it were. If so, the system of values ought to be consistent with this form of society and the psychological attitudes that go with it. Traditional Japanese values do indeed stress the subordination of the individual to the collectivity—family, hamlet, corporation, and so on.

Specifically, those in leadership positions—parents, employers, patrons—must feel a strong sense of responsibility for the actions as well as the welfare of their subordinates. The subordinates, in turn, are required to reciprocate by showing loyalty and devotion to their superiors. Thus the obligation to maintain interdependent reciprocal obligations is codified in the sense of *giri*. As George De Vos notes, the "maintenance of obligations is still an essential part of Japanese life. Although the fulfillment of obligations does not play the primary role it played in the past, any careful examination of a professional community or a business organization will reveal that networks of obligation remain an extremely important part of professional and economic intercommunication and negotiation.'"[7]

The bonds of obligation, as De Vos suggests, have been weakening, but they have by no means disappeared. De Vos remarks that "changes are occurring in modern Japanese, especially in those under thirty, but it is not yet possible to determine whether the ultimate direction taken by Japanese culture in defining role relationships will be completely congruent with that of Western modernization."[8] In other words, traditional values relating to dependency and inter-personal relationships are slowly being eroded, but no single alternative system of values has yet emerged.

The erosion of traditional values, of course, has some important political implications. A convenient way to begin the analysis is to consider the analogous situation in Great Britain. Various explanations have been given for the existence of Tory workers, who constitute about a third of the working class. Frank Parkin's explanation, which has a good deal to commend it, is that the core values of British society are represented by conservatism. He notes that "political choice is an index of individuals' commitments not merely to parties and programmes, but to a wide range of social values; for obviously, political allegiances are to an important extent a reflection of the values men subscribe to in areas of life outside the realm of politics."[9] According to this view, the so-called Tory workers are voting in accordance with social values, and those workers who vote for Labour are indicating "deviance" from the dominant system. Thus, the reasoning goes, "electoral support for Socialism will occur predominantly where individuals are involved in normative sub-systems which serve as 'barriers' to the dominant values of society."[10] An example of such a subsystem is residence in working-class neighborhoods.

When we turn to the Japanese case, it is obvious that the

Liberal Democratic party is closely related to the dominant social values, that is, it relies on traditional reciprocal interpersonal ties in relating itself to the electorate. One can think of the Liberal Democratic party as the political expression of traditional values, and of those who do not support it as to some extent "deviant." Hence, in part, the fortunes of the Liberal Democratic party will hinge on what happens to the dominant social values.

Some empirical evidence sheds light on this matter. The researchers at the Institute of Mathematical Statistics took from the national character surveys a set of sixteen questions that in their judgment were related to traditional moral and social values. Individuals' responses to these questions were scored on a scale from 0 to 16—the higher the score, the stronger the preference for traditional values. The distribution of responses fell in a kind of bell-shaped curve but skewed toward the lower end. The responses clustered around scores 4 to 8, with the average around 6. A second group of ten questions, which presumably were the opposite of those in the first set, was designed to measure rejection of traditional values. Party support was then plotted against these two scales. Although the differences among the parties were not large, the overall tendency was quite clear: the Liberal Democratic party fell at one end, the traditional, and the Communist party occupied the other extreme, as can be seen in figure 4.[11] Traditional values, then, do appear to be related to party support. Quite clearly, however, other variables must also be involved.

A second variable is social class—a variable that most Marxist analysts would put at the top of the list. One indicator of the strength of class as a factor in politics is the awareness of social class and the relationship of such awareness to political ideology and political party preference. A survey of male voters in Tokyo carried out in 1967, which is cited by Yasuda Saburo, suggests that awareness of class and attitudes toward socialism are related, at least in this sample. Respondents were asked, "If one were to divide Japanese society into three classes—working class, middle class, and capitalist class—where do you think you belong?"

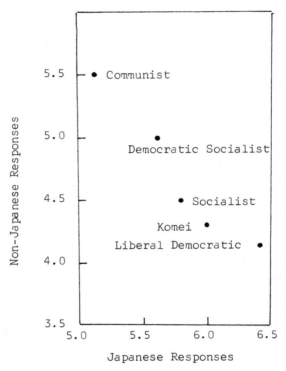

Figure 4. Relationship Between Japanese Values and Party Support

The socialism question was phrased as follows: "There is a view that 'In order to make Japanese society better, the way in which society is organized must be changed to socialism.' Are you in favor of this view or opposed?" The results are given in table 4-3. As is evident from table 4-3, respondents who perceived themselves to be a member of the working class expressed more favorable attitudes toward socialism than those who identified with the capitalist class; those who saw themselves as middle-class took an intermediate position. Thus ideological considerations appear to be present to some extent. But it is worth noting that only three out of ten who said they were working-class expressed prosocialist attitudes and that four out of ten expressed negative feelings toward socialism. It would seem that in this sample at least, working-class awareness and prosocialist sentiment were present but not pronounced.

Table 4-3

Perceived Class Position and Attitudes
Toward Socialism

Class identification	Against socialism	Neither for nor against	socialism	Total	N
Working class	43.2%	26.7%	30.1%	100.0%	359
Middle class	58.0	21.4	20.6	100.0	257
Capitalist class	70.3	18.9	10.8	100.0	37

p< 0.001

Source: Yasuda Saburo. <u>Gendai Nihon no Kaikyu Ishiki</u>
(Class Consciousness in Contemporary Japan).
Tokyo, 1973, p. 88.

The next step is to look at the relationship between favorable attitudes toward socialism and party support. Do those who favor socialism support leftist parties? In general, the answer seems to be yes, as can be seen in table 4-4. The data in table 4-4 show that almost seven out of ten respondents who agreed that socialism should be introduced to improve Japan supported either the Socialist or Communist party, and that half of those who disagreed supported the ruling party. Those who refused to take a position tended to favor the Liberal Democratic party or supported no party. Almost one out of five who opposed socialism, however, supported either the Socialist or Communist party, and a little more than one out of seven prosocialists supported the conservatives. Thus working-class identification and prosocialist point of view contribute to support for the Socialist and Communist parties, but other factors are clearly at work here.

Table 4-4

Socialism and Party Support

Attitude toward socialism	Party support					N
	No party	LDP	Komei	Dem.- Soc.	Socialist, Communist	
For socialism	10.1%	15.4%	5.3%	10.7%	58.5%	169
Against socialism	15.9	50.0	2.4	12.5	19.2	328
Neither	29.3	31.9	3.9	14.0	21.0	157

$p < 0.001$

Source: Yasuda. Gendai Nihon no Kaikyu Ishiki, p. 90.

Another way to approach this problem of class voting is to use a measure suggested by Robert Alford in his study of voting in Anglo-American systems.[12] For this, we can cite more recent data than were available to Watanuki when he wrote his essay. These figures were obtained by Ikeuchi Hajime et al. in their 1967 national survey of political attitudes.[13] What Alford has called a "crude measure" of class voting is obtained by "subtracting the percentage of persons in non-manual occupations voting for Left parties from the percentage of manual workers for such parties." Using Ikeuchi's data, we get the following index. International comparisons are difficult to make and can sometimes be misleading, but one can note, for whatever it is worth, that the difference between the two groups of workers in table 4-5 is fairly small compared to figures Alford gives for Britain (40), Australia (33), and the United States (16). It is somewhat larger than Canada (8) and appears to be at least consistent with what was stated earlier about the class variable. It is also consistent with the impression one gets that the Japanese polity is not characterized by sharp class cleavages.

Table 4-5

Index of Class Voting

Manual workers for Socialist & Communist parties	48.1%
Nonmanual workers for Socialist & Communist parties	35.8
difference	12.3

Source: Ikeuchi Hajime et al. Shimin Ishiki no Kenkyu
         (A Study of Citizen Attitudes). Tokyo, 1974,
         p. 427.
         Note: The percentages were calculated from
         Table 6-78. "Romu" were classified as manual
         workers, "jimu, hambai, and sabisu" as nonman-
         ual. Data show support and not necessarily
         voting practice.

A brief look at other important groups—professional and managerial, the self-employed, and farmers and fishermen—will round out the picture. In these instances, the data were obtained by the Institute of Mathematical Statistics as part of its continuing study of Japanese national character.[14]

There is an interesting contrast between the professional and managerial groups, as can be seen from the table 4-6. More than half the professionals in the sample supported one or the other of Japan's opposition parties. It has been reported that "professionals, like blue-collar workers in large enterprises, identify with and have a sense of solidarity with the working class. Many of them blame society for the existence of poverty, rather than the individual, while many

of those in the managerial group, as is true with the self-
employed, take the opposite position."[15] Those in both
professional and managerial categories are generally highly
educated. Education, we may speculate, may have tended to
make the former more socially conscious, and economic interests may have forced the latter to adopt a more conservative stance.

Table 4-6

Individuals in Professional and Managerial
Position & Party Support, 1968

Party	Professional		Managerial	
Opposition	39	46.5%	10	17.5%
Ruling	29	34.5	36	63.2
No party	15	17.9	8	14.0
Other	1	1.1	3	5.3
	84	100.0%	57	100.0%

Source: Tokeisuri Kenkyujo. Kokuminsei no Kenkyu
(A Study of National Character), 1968.
Tokyo, 1969, p. 143. (Numbers have been
recalculated from percentages given in the
table on p. 143).

Finally, one would expect that independent businessmen
and farmers do not support opposition parties but back the
Liberal Democrats, who are committed to the capitalist
order. Some 1968 data bear this out, as indicated in table 4-7.
More than half the independent businessmen and farmers
favored the ruling party. But a little more than one out of six
indicated support for the opposition parties, and an equal
number apparently did not have a commitment to any party.

In summary, class obviously has some influence on the
party supported: independent businessmen, farmers, and
those in managerial positions tend to favor the Liberal

Democratic party, a stance consistent with their economic interests. Manual workers, by contrast, lean to the Left, which is also consistent with their economic interests, since they work for wages (but as we have seen, their support for the Left is rather moderate). In short, class cleavages do exist and are reflected to some extent in the political parties, but the relationship is not as strong as one might believe. The "renegades" who desert their class and join the opposition, together with those who profess to have no party preference, sometimes represent a sizable minority (40 percent or more).

Table 4-7

Party Support Among Businessmen and Farmers, 1968

Party	Businessmen		Farmers	
Opposition	61	17.9%	76	16.0%
Ruling	198	58.1	270	56.8
No party	61	17.9	86	18.1
Other	21	6.1	43	9.1
	341	100.0%	475	100.0%

Source: Tokeisuri Kenkyujo. <u>Kokuminsei no Kenkyu</u>, p. 143.

Social Networks

The third and last variable to be considered—after class and party—is the influence of social networks. It was suggested earlier that the relationship between class and party can be explained better in relation to the idea of frame as a mediating variable. But first it is necessary to digress and take up the question of political socialization.

Some analysts of American and European democratic systems associate the stability of democracy with party identification, which they regard as a key factor. The argument runs as follows. If a democracy is to achieve stability, citizens must have a strong commitment to a particular political party to enable that party to survive over time. Short-lived and ephemeral parties are detrimental to democratic stability. Moreover, party loyalty affects other attitudes and behavior relating to politics, making for more consistency in individuals' perception of and response to political issues. Thus, party allegiance makes it possible for individuals to join with like-minded people to work for the attainment of the collective good. Party loyalty, like other political phenomena, is learned. Probably the most important agency for socializing individuals for participation in political life is the family. There one initially acquires a sense of party allegiance, which is nurtured by the family as well as by other social agencies, such as peer groups, schools, and the like. Party identification is particularly strong and enduring when it has been transmitted from one generation to succeeding generations. According to this school of thought, then, party allegiance, once acquired early in life, will not change very easily.

Unfortunately, not much is known about political socialization in Japan. The subject has not received the kind of scholarly attention that it deserves. A discussion of the existing state of knowledge is contained in Ellis Krauss's pioneering study of radical students.[16]

In brief, Krauss and others found that parents who supported leftist parties, particularly the Socialist and Communist parties, appeared "to transmit their party preferences to their children more often than do LDP supporters."[17] Krauss reasons that supporters of leftist parties should be more highly politicized than conservatives and that therefore they were more likely to transmit partisan feelings to their children. His data, however, do not support this hypothesis. "Progressive parents who did not discuss politics with their children were as likely to have children who shared their party preferences as those who did discuss politics. Parents who did not support a Left party were likely to have offspring whose party preference was different from theirs whether they discussed politics in the family or not."[18] His conclusion is that the "family's role as a direct transmitter of party identification, as an agent of politicization, and as a model of political behavior seems quite limited."[19] If the family does not transmit party loyalty, what does? Krauss's response is "other influences in their environments." "Later experiences," he notes, "lead to the acquisition of a left-wing orientation or identification with a primary or secondary group other than the family which is left-leaning."[20] A good example of identification with a left-leaning group is membership in a labor union. The union may be looked upon as kind of frame. Therefore, we will take up the union as a mediating influence in the first of several case studies.

Case One: Unions

Over the years there has been a slow movement of industry away from the leading industrial centers around Tokyo and Osaka and toward the less-developed rural regions of Japan. Factories and plants have been established in small towns and cities, and young men and women who had been born and raised in farm villages have found employment in these enterprises. Because of the relatively well developed transportation system, such factory workers have often been able to live at home and commute to their place of work.

Thus an individual was not only socialized in a family that was probably politically conservative but continued to live in a conservative environment. Yet, as a factory worker, the same individual became a member of a labor union. His or her environment has changed somewhat, but not completely. Socialization theory based on Western experience suggests that the factory worker will continue to support the conservative party because of the transmission of party loyalty through the family. Krauss's hypothesis, by contrast, suggests that the factory worker who commutes probably supports a radical party.

In 1957 a team headed by Nakamura Kikuo collected data (now somewhat dated, unfortunately) in the course of a survey of several villages in Mie prefecture.[21] Nakamura and his associates interviewed three groups of people: (1) village residents, (2) commuters who worked in nearby factories, and (3) residents of a company-owned housing unit. The last were probably not local inhabitants but those who had moved in from the outside.

Table 4-8

Comparison of Party Supporters Among
Commuters and Noncommuters

Party	Commuters		Villagers		Company housing residents	
Lib-Democratic	6	12.0%	39	42.3%	2	11.1%
Socialist	33	66.0	15	16.3	12	66.7
Communist	0	00.0	0	00.0	0	00.0
Other	5	10.0	15	16.3	3	16.7
Can't say	1	2.0	4	4.3	1	5.5
Haven't decided	2	4.0	13	14.1	0	0.0
Don't know party affiliation of candidate	0	0.0	1	1.0	0	0.0
Don't know	3	6.0	5	5.7	0	0.0
Totals	50	100.0%	92	100.0%	18	100.0%

Source: Nakamura Kikuo (ed.). <u>Nihon ni okeru Seito to Seiji Ishiki</u> (Political Parties in Japan and Political Attitudes). Tokyo, 1971, p. 44.

Among the interview questions was one on party support: "If today an election for the House of Representatives were held, what party's candidate would you vote for?" The responses are given in table 4-8. The data indicate that commuters favor the Socialist party by a substantial margin, thirty-three out of fifty, which stands in contrast to the villagers, who, as expected, support the Liberal Democratic party by a sizable margin of thirty-nine to fifteen. Nakamura also reanalyzed the data, controlling for age, on the theory that younger commuters might prefer the Socialists. He looked at both the commuters and villagers aged twenty to forty, and the two samples still retained the difference noted above.[22] Thus, union membership, rather than age, may have accounted for the different political party orientations of commuters and villagers, although unknown factors could be present here, too.

Nakamura also sensed that the left-leaning proclivities of the commuters represented a source of tension in their families, since the other members would probably be inclined to vote for a Liberal Democratic candidate. He and his associates, however, were unable to study this problem systematically since the respondents were randomly chosen individuals. In other words, the unit of analysis was individuals rather than families or other small groups. He did observe, however, that there were cases in which the factory worker picked up information about elections from fellow workers and passed it on to family members and friends.[23]

An interesting question is to what extent union membership and the prosocialist attitudes associated with it were rooted in radical ideology. Nakamura found evidence that commuters tended to be more politically conscious than noncommuters, but it is difficult to say whether the two groups had significant ideological differences. Nakamura asked respondents in one of the villages to react to three statements about what the Socialist party ought to do:

1.   The Socialist party ought to promote the interests of the working class even if it has to bring about a revolution.
2.   The Socialist party ought to promote the interests of the working class within the framework of the present parliamentary system.
3.   The Socialist party ought to promote the interests not only of the working class but also of the peasants and small and medium-sized businesses.

The response to each of these questions is given in table 4-9. Of particular interest are the responses by commuters, who are mostly Socialists. They do not believe that their party should become revolutionary but prefer it to take the parliamentary road and even to broaden its base to include peasants and owners of small and medium-sized businesses. Thus, their views are quite moderate: if we compare the commuters to the peasants in the sample, there is very little difference in the pattern of the responses. In short, the commuters do not appear to be very different ideologically from those in other groups.

This should not be altogether surprising. After all, the people who commute to nearby factories were born and raised in essentially a conservative environment and, indeed, continue to live in such surroundings. Thus, there must be some factor other than ideology that moves commuters to vote for the Socialists. A plausible hypothesis is that their voting behavior represents an act of solidarity with their fellow union members. Indeed, Nakamura notes that working in a modern factory necessitates adjustments on the part of commuters who grew up in a traditional community and that this need to adjust arouses a desire to conform to the group attitudes that prevail in the factory. Group conformity, moreover, was reinforced by the fact that commuters often saw one another on their way to and from the factory

and on these occasions sometimes discussed politics. In
addition, there were opportunities for them to get together
outside of the work situation in discussion groups and other
forms of social activity.[24] In short, the elements that went
into the creation of union solidarity were probably not all
that different from those that form the basis of village
solidarity. In this particular case, one might think of union
solidarity as an extension of village solidarity. For commuters, therefore, there were two social networks, the village and
the union. The empirical evidence shows that at least in the
case of national elections, the social network represented
by the union took precedence over that of the village.

Table 4-9

Preferred Role of the Socialist Party
for Peasants and Commuters (Males)

Role	Preference	Peasants	Commuters	Others
Revolutionary	Approve	20%	17%	14%
party	Disapprove	37	65	36
	Can't say;			
	don't know	43	18	50
		100%	100%	100%
		(N=63)	(N=55)	(N=36)
Parliamentary	Approve	41%	60%	36%
party	Disapprove	23	13	17
	Can't say;			
	don't know	36	27	47
		100%	100%	100%
		(N=63)	(N=55)	(N=36)
Working class,	Approve	86%	89%	75%
peasant & small	Disapprove	0	4	3
business	Can't say;			
party	don't know	14	7	22
		100%	100%	100%
		(N=63)	(N=55)	(N=36)

Source: Nakamura (ed.). Nihon ni okeru Seito to Seiji
        Ishiki. p. 232.

Perhaps one could even say that in behavior the union was dominant, but that in political views the village continued to exercise its sway. Moreover, the divergence between behavior and political attitudes may represent a Japanese response to cross-pressures. According to cross-pressure theory, commuters might have been expected to withdraw from politics because they were caught between conservative pressure coming from their families and the village and radical pressure from the union. But the empirical evidence does not indicate that this was the case; if anything, the commuters were more active politically than the non-commuters.

Another inference can be made about the relationship between behavior and ideology. That is, unions in urban and metropolitan settings ought to be somewhat different from those in rural areas: in all likelihood, urban unions cannot use the primordial group loyalties and intense personalized interaction patterns that are found in rural areas as the basis of union solidarity. Urban workers have probably come from various parts of the country and therefore probably do not have a common set of values, life experiences, and friendship patterns that are found in unions in small towns. Thus, urban unions presumably have a lower degree of solidarity. But to make up for this, they may well have a strong commitment to radical ideology. These notions can be expressed as a hypothesis: labor unions in rural areas are strong in solidarity but weak in radical ideology, and unions in urban settings are weak in solidarity but strong in radical ideology. The issue will have to remain unsettled because we lack the data to test this proposition directly.

In any case, there ought to be some kind of relationship between labor union membership and support for leftist parties. After all, it is the official policy of the two major labor union federations, namely, Sohyo and Domei, to support the Socialist and Democratic Socialist parties, respectively. Of course, the rank and file may not choose to follow official union policy in politics.

One way to examine this relationship is to compare the number of workers enrolled in unions with the votes cast for the Socialist and Democratic Socialist parties. The data are as follows:

1975 Union membership (in millions)		1976 Votes (in millions)	
Sohyo	4.57	Socialist	11.7
Domei	2.26	Democrat Socialist	3.5
Other	5.76		
Total	12.59	Total	15.2

The statistics suggest that there is a rough relationship between membership in Sohyo and Domei and votes for the Socialist and Democratic Socialist parties, respectively. If we assume that most union members probably can influence their family members to vote as they do, then the vote ought to be much higher, since presumably these parties also get support from non-working-class voters as well as from working-class individuals who do not belong to unions.

One reason for the unexpectedly low vote is that both the Communist and Clean Government parties siphon off some support. This is suggested by an analysis made by the *Yomiuri* newspaper, which correlated the percentage of unionized workers within the labor force with party support. The results are given in table 4-10. The data in it suggest that the Socialist party has met with considerable competition from both the Communist and Clean Government parties in the most industrialized areas. It also meets competition in the least industrialized areas from the ruling party. Therefore, it does better in the moderately industrialized sections of the country.

Table 4-10

Relationship Between Percentage of Unionized Workers
in Labor Force and Party Support, 1972

Labor force: percent unionized	Vote				
	Soc.	D-Soc.	Communist	Komei	LDP
30% and up	21.7%	9.7%	16.8%	14.3%	33.7%
27-29	20.3	10.2	11.7	9.5	42.1
25-26	24.8	5.9	8.8	5.7	49.6
23-24	21.9	4.1	7.0	6.1	56.7
22 and less	20.0	0.2	5.5	4.7	59.1

Source: Yomiuri Shimbun. Senkyo o Tettei Bunsekisuru
(A Thorough Analysis of Elections). Tokyo,
1975, p. 34.

There is also some evidence that unionized workers, like
many other voters, have tended to eschew identification with
any particular party. According to a survey of 1,168 unionized workers made in 1973, 54.1 percent of those interviewed
stated that they supported no particular political party.[25]
When pressed, however, 44.2 percent of the "no party" group
said that they inclined toward the Left.

Case Two: Work Environment

As was mentioned earlier, one of the notable features of the
Japanese economy is the relatively large number of self-
employed. This is an aspect of the so-called dual economy.
Large-scale industrialization has not completely eliminated
small and medium-sized business enterprises, but instead
has incorporated them into the economic structure through
the subcontracting system. Of immediate concern to this
study are the political attitudes, especially party preferences,

Table 4-11

Party Preferences of White Collar Workers
in Large and Small Establishments

Party	Large establishments		Small establishments	
Ruling	52	24.2%	62	43.4%
Opposition	110	51.2	54	37.8
Other	6	2.7	6	4.2
No party	47	21.9	21	14.6
Totals	215	100.0%	143	100.0%

Source: Tokeisuri Kenkyujo. <u>Kokuminsei no Kenkyu</u>, p. 143.

of those employed in small and medium-sized enterprises.

Our theory is that politics in Japan is highly personalized and that those in patron positions are often able to exert considerable influence over their clients. It was previously shown that independent businessmen strongly favor the Liberal Democratic party. One would expect, then, that in small business establishments, where the owner-manager personally oversees his employees with a firm but paternalistic hand, the employees are likely to adopt political attitudes that are in tune with those of the employer.

To test this proposition, we can again use data from the national character survey undertaken in 1968. Party preferences of white-collar workers in large and small establishments are given in table 4-11. White-collar workers in large establishments favor the opposition parties over the Liberal Democratic party by a ratio of more than two to one, and about one out of five do not support any particular party. By contrast, white-collar workers employed in small business firms are more conservative, and the proportion of those who do not support any party is smaller than in large firms. Thus, the work environment appears to affect party choice among white-collar workers.

Essentially the same picture emerges among blue-collar workers employed in large and small establishments. The data are presented in table 4-12. Blue-collar workers in large firms are noticeably more opposition-oriented than their counterparts in small establishments. Again the work environment seems to affect party preference.

Table 4-12

Party Preferences of Blue Collar Workers
in Large and Small Establishments

Party	Large establishments		Small establishments	
Ruling	72	24.9%	71	30.9%
Opposition	136	47.0	85	37.0
Other	17	5.9	16	6.9
No party	64	22.2	58	25.2
	289	100.0%	230	100.0%

Source: Tokeisuri Kenkyujo. <u>Kokuminsei no Kenkyu</u>.
         p. 143.

Case Three: Work Autonomy

Between 1961 and 1962, Miyake Ichiro and his associates carried out extensive surveys in Uji, a city near Kyoto. It was a panel survey in which essentially the same set of respondents was interviewed on five different occasions spread out over a one-year period.[26] Miyake discovered during the course of these interviews that a certain number of these respondents had changed jobs and that under certain circumstances the change in job was accompanied by a change in political party affiliation.[27] Since this phenomenon appeared after the surveys were taken, he was unable to follow up on this interesting problem. His questionnaire contained no items that would throw light on this matter.

But the phenomenon did intrigue the investigators, and Miyake includes a short discussion of it in his massive study of Uji. In essence he believes that two factors are at work. One is a person's work autonomy, that is, whether he works without supervision or supervises others. The second factor is an individual's belief that he is part of what Miyake calls the "mainstream," that is, the establishment or the established order.[28] Under this latter category come those who represent authority, for instance, policemen and government officials.

Politically, one who works without supervision or supervises others, or one who considers himself to be part of the establishment tends to support the Liberal Democratic party. Those who are supervised by others or do not consider themselves part of the establishment tend to prefer the opposition, leftist parties. When Miyake's respondents changed jobs and moved from one category to another, the result seemed to be a shift in party support in the direction indicated here. Since he had no data that got at this variable directly, Miyake ingeniously tried to deal with it indirectly by classifying occupations along this supervisor-supervised dimension. He found, for example, that there was a correlation between this variable and party support. The results are given in table 4-13. As the table shows, 43 percent of those whom Miyake inferred to have supervisory positions supported the Liberal Democratic party, and only 9 percent of those who presumably were supervised preferred the same party. The situation is exactly reversed when it comes to the Democratic Socialist and Socialist parties. These parties are favored markedly by those who are supervised.

Table 4-13

Party Support in Relation to Supervisory
or Supervised Work

Party	Supervisory	Supervised
Liberal Democratic	43%	9%
Democratic Socialist	8	13
Socialist	21	59
Communist	2	1
Independent, not applicable	26	18
	100%	100%
n=171		

Source: Miyake Y. et al. <u>Kotonaru Reberu no Senkyo ni okeru Tohyo Kodo no Kenkyu</u> (Study of Electoral Behavior in Elections at Various Levels), Tokyo, 1967, p. 127.

Miyake also made what is admittedly not a very scientific survey of a few taxicab drivers, with some rather provocative results. The sample included forty drivers, divided equally between those who drove their own cabs and those who worked for a cab company. According to the work autonomy theory, the owner-drivers are conservative, and the employee-drivers are radical. The results are given in table 4-14. The results are consistent with the theory. Owner-drivers support either the Liberal Democratic party or the moderate Democratic Socialists, and employee-drivers prefer the Socialists or Communists. Miyake notes further that many of the owner-drivers used to work for cab companies before they became independent drivers and that during this earlier period they supported leftist parties. There is probably no appreciable difference in income or class position between these two groups of drivers, so Miyake reasons that the supervisor-supervised variable must be at work here.

Table 4-14

Status of Taxi Drivers and Party Support

Party	Owner Drivers	Employee Drivers
Liberal Democratic	50%	0%
Democratic Socialist	40	0
Socialist	10	75
Communist	0	25
	100%	100%
n=20		

Source: Miyake Y., et al. <u>Kotonaru Reberu no Senkyo</u>
<u>ni okeru Tohyo Kodo no Kenkyu,</u> p. 120.

Concluding Remarks

We began with the notion that traditional values, social class, and social networks are related to political cleavages in contemporary Japan. The empirical data examined in this chapter appear to confirm that these three variables do indeed have some bearing on cleavages. Quite clearly, some of these variables tend to reinforce each other. For example, an individual who rejects traditional values, belongs to the working class, and is a member of a labor union ought to be a supporter of one of the opposition parties. It is conceivable, however, that the variables may sometimes work against each other. For instance, a blue-collar employee of a small firm run by a paternalistic and politically conservative businessman may well support the Liberal Democratic party. In this case, social class and social networks could be in conflict, and the "pull" of the social networks would probably be stronger than that of social class. In any case, if at least three variables help account for cleavages, then the analysis of cleavages can be quite complex. The data currently available probably do not permit fairly precise calculations about the relative weights that should be assigned to these variables. Research designed especially to investigate this problem is needed.

5
Economic Growth and the Party in Power

According to American political folklore, the party in power is helped by prosperity and hurt by the lack of it. When times are good, the electorate is likely to reward those in office by voting for them in the next election. When economic activity declines and people begin to feel the painful effects of declining profits and rising unemployment, the electorate is likely to punish the incumbents.

The decade of the 1960s was an era of unprecedented economic growth in Japan. Growth was the watchword in all of the advanced economies of the world, but the Japanese rate of growth was particularly spectacular and persistent. The gross national product, the standard measure of economic activity, rose from $53 billion in 1961 to $197 billion in 1970, a growth rate of almost 16 percent a year. As might be expected economic growth changed consumption patterns, life-styles, and the occupational composition of the population. It also affected politics, but not in the direction one would have guessed. Instead of profiting from prosperity in the form of enhanced support from a grateful electorate, the Liberal Democratic party, the ruling party, actually lost ground to the opposition parties. Its share of the vote in the House of Representatives election fell from 57.8

percent in the 1960 election to 47.6 percent in the 1969 election, or just over 10 percent during a nine-year period. If it was any consolation, the Liberal Democrats could also note that the Socialist party, the second largest party, suffered the same fate, falling from 32.9 percent in 1960 to 21.4 percent in 1969.

In the 1970s, the rate of economic growth slowed down appreciably, especially for a short period after the so-called oil shock in 1973. The Japanese now appear to be reconciled to a lower level of growth, but they are still expected to do quite well by international standards and maintain about 6 percent growth a year for the rest of the decade.

Meanwhile, the erosion of support for the Liberal Democratic party continued in elections held in 1972 and 1976. In the 1972 election, the party won 46.9 percent of the popular vote, and in 1976 it won 41.8 percent, a rather sharp drop. Thus, there was, contrary to political folklore, an inverse correlation between economic growth and voter support for the ruling party.

How does one explain this? As is often true of political phenomena, there appears to be no single cause to which one can point. But the investment model does provide some interesting clues. For example, social networks and benefits are important elements in the model, and it is possible to look at the decline in support for the ruling party partly in terms of these elements. First, population shifts resulting from economic growth have put many individuals into different social networks, which in turn has affected electoral turnout and party affiliation. Population shifts have also aggravated the problem of underrepresentation of urban interests in the House of Representatives, which has led urban dwellers to feel that the ruling party has not been sufficiently responsive to their needs. Second, the trend toward privatization, especially among young people, has worked to reduce electoral turnout, which has put the ruling party at a disadvantage. Third, the increasing concern about

the pollution and inflation that have come with prosperity
has probably resulted in some shifts in the kinds of benefits
sought, again resulting in a movement of voters away from
the Liberal Democratic party.

Population Shifts

Sustained economic growth in the 1960s had some interesting demographic consequences. Prosperity was achieved
by accelerating industrialization, which in turn was made
possible by a rather massive shift in the labor force from the
rural areas to the great industrial centers located in a belt
extending west from the Tokyo-Yokohama area to the
Osaka-Kobe complex and extending along the Inland Sea to
northern Kyushu. Some idea of the magnitude of this shift
may be gleaned from table 5-1.

Table 5-1

Urban Shift of the Work Force, 1960-1970

Migration from nonurban to urban areas	12,889,000
Migration from urban to nonurban areas	7,267,000
Difference	5,622,000
Total migration	20,156,000

Source: Okazaki Yoichi, "Saikin ni okeru Jinko Rodo no
          Chiiki-teki Bumpu no Henka ni tsuite" (On the
          Regional Distribution of the Labor Force in
          Recent Times), Nihon Rodo Kyokai Zasshi, No.
          170 (May 1970), p. 27.

Altogether some 20 million persons, or about one-fifth of
the population, migrated during this decade. More than 12
million moved from the rural areas to the heavily populated
industrialized areas, and a large number of these migrants
were young men and women who left home in search of new
economic opportunities. Of course, not all of them stayed

in the big cities. Some found it difficult to adjust and returned to the communities where they had grown up. Japanese commentators have called this phenomenon, "U-turn." Others reversed the process and went from the city to the country. They very likely included older people who had retired. In any case, as table 5-1 shows, there was a net increase of about 5.6 million people in the metropolitan areas and many of these were young people. Population shifts have continued in the 1970s, but at a markedly slower pace.

Since these young people presumably were raised in those sections of the country where the Liberal Democratic party is strong, one might assume that they had been inculcated with conservative political attitudes. At least, that is what political socialization theory would suggest. But as we tried to show in chapter 4, party loyalty does not appear to be inculcated in Japanese politics to any great degree, and more important than socialization, it seems, is the nature of an individual's social networks.

One of the consequences of migration on this scale is that millions of people have been taken from a village social and political environment and placed in urban centers. At least two theories seek to explain what is likely to happen when this takes place. According to the mobilization model, urbanization leads to enhanced political participation because of more exposure to communications, more stimulation from other people, and the development of beliefs and personality traits more conducive to increased participation.

The alternative model—the decline of community model—stands in opposition to the first and predicts exactly the reverse, that is, less participation. As Norman Nie and Sidney Verba put it, "In the small town the community is of a manageable size. Citizens can know the ropes of politics, know whom to contact, and know each other so that they can form political groups. In the larger unit politics is more complicated, impersonal and distant."[1] Nie and Verba then compare data from seven countries, including Japan, and conclude that "data support an interpretation that the nature of the community does make a difference in participation over and above the effects of the characteristics of the individual citizens who live there. The difference it makes is related to the degree to which the community is isolated enough so that the citizen has a well-defined political unit within which to participate."[2]

Quite clearly, the decline of community model is the correct one for contemporary Japanese politics. In rural areas there are usually well-established social networks that are "plugged into" politics, but the situation in the cities is usually not structured so clearly. Social networks exist, but they may not be well developed, and they may not be particularly relevant to politics.

We can illustrate this point by citing the results of a survey of civic attitudes, which was a part of the multinational research effort from which Nie and Verba drew their data. One of the questions asked sought to determine the perceived "distance" between citizens and local administrative officials in Japan. Respondents were asked to state whether in their opinion they would need an introduction if they needed to contact such an official. The responses listed by place of residence are given in table 5-2. As it shows, those who live in towns and villages tended to feel that they could go and see an official without first getting an introduction from someone who knew him personally. By contrast, almost two-thirds of the city respondents felt that they needed an introduction.

The survey also sought to determine whether those who said that they needed an introduction felt that such introductions would be easy or difficult to obtain. The results are summarized in table 5-3. Again, most of those who live in towns and villages, as compared to residents of cities and metropolitan areas, perceive that it is fairly easy to get introductions to achieve smooth access to local government officials. I would argue that these differences in perceptions can be attributed to the differences between urban and rural social networks. Life in cities tends to be more anonymous.

If the decline of community model is valid for Japan, then the cities that grew tremendously as a result of an influx

Table 5-2

Need for Introduction When Contacting
Officials (by place of residence)

Residence	Needed	It depends	Not needed	Other	Don't know	N
Towns,villages	36.5%	2.0%	47.5%	3.1%	10.9%	806
Cities	52.9	4.2	27.9	3.3	11.7	1345
7 metropolitan cities	66.0	4.5	12.1	8.3	9.1	506

Source: Ikeuchi Hajime et al. Shimin Ishiki no Kenkyu,
         p. 325.

Table 5-3

Ease or Difficulty in Getting Introductions
to Local Officials (by place of residence)

Residence	Easy	Not so easy	Very difficult	Other	Don't know	N
Towns, villages	51.0%	28.7%	16.8%	--	3.5%	310
Cities	43.0	30.5	20.6	1.3	4.7	768
7 metropolitan cities	31.4	33.3	30.0	1.7	3.6	357

Source: Ikeuchi Hajime et al. Shimin Ishiki no Kenkyu,
         p. 331.

of migrants should be characterized by especially low electoral participation rates. Recent migrants would not have had time to get acquainted with many people or to get to know the "ropes" of politics. They would feel more isolated than they felt in the rural areas. The result, one would hypothesize, would be lower voting rates.

To test this hypothesis, we calculated the increase in the number of eligible voters by prefecture (those with large in-migration have large increases in eligible voters) and compared the data with the percentage of eligible voters actually voting during the 1976 House of Representatives election. The results can be seen in figure 5-1.

The scatterplot indicates that there is an inverse relationship between an increase in the number of eligible voters and electoral participation. Those prefectures that had large increases in the number of eligible voters generally had lower rates of participation.

Electoral participation, in turn, appears to be related to Liberal Democratic party strength. Since the Liberal Democratic party has no party organization to speak of, it must depend on other mechanisms for securing the vote. The primary mechanism is the personal tie, direct or indirect, that has been established between the population and the candidates who run for office with the party endorsement. The tie is direct where the candidate has created so-called support organizations, which are essentially political machines committed to the candidate's support. The tie is more indirect where candidates form alliances with local politicians at various levels, politicians who, in turn, are in a position to mobilize patron-client clusters.[3] Under the circumstances, it is not surprising that the party flourishes in the kind of social milieu that is congenial to personalized relationships, namely, rural hamlets and villages, where voters can be more easily mobilized for the conservative cause. Thus, there is a relationship between the level of electoral participation and the vote for the Liberal Democratic

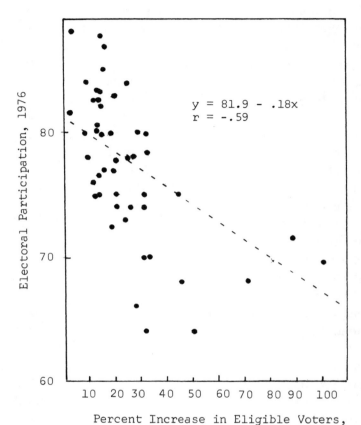

Figure 5-1.   Relationship Between Increase in Eligible Voters and Electoral
Participation

party, as is suggested in figure 5-2. The relationship between
these two variables is positive, that is, high participation
seems to go together with more votes for the Liberal Democratic party.

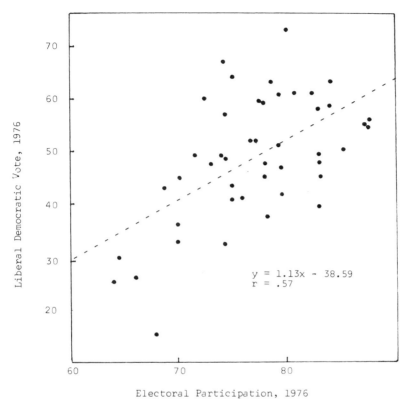

Figure 5-2. Relationship Between Electoral Participation and Vote for the Liberal Democratic Party

Since the increase in the number of eligible voters is inversely related to electoral participation, as shown in figure 5-1, one can infer that urban in-migration has not benefited the Liberal Democratic party, despite the fact that millions of young people born and raised in the heartland of Liberal Democratic strength moved to the urban and metropolitan districts. One way to check this is to see whether there is any relationship in the prefectures between an increase in

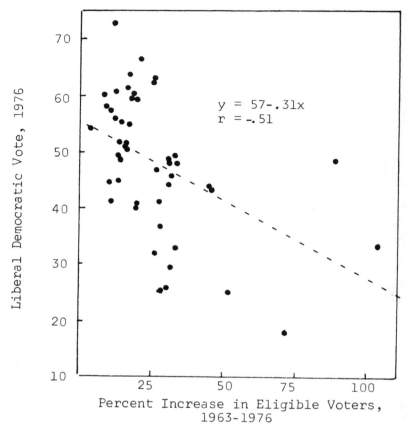

Figure 5-3.   Relationship Between Increase in Eligible Voters and Vote for
the Liberal Democratic Party

the number of eligible voters and changes in the vote for the
Liberal Democratic party candidates between 1963 and 1976.
The relationship is shown in figure 5-3. The dots in the scatterplot are fairly scattered, which suggests that the association, which is negative, is only moderate. The linear regression coefficient is -0.51. In other words, the Liberal Democratic party tended to do less well in prefectures that had
large increases in the number of eligible voters. (Actually
the coefficient is fairly high when one considers that it is

based on ecological variables rather than on individual attitudes.)

Another way to approach this same problem is to look at the electoral districts to see to what extent voters in each district are overrepresented or underrepresented. We have already noted that the system works against urban residents. Electoral districts have been ranked according to the number of eligible voters per representative (as of September 1975), and the resulting list clearly brings out the tremendous disparities that exist.[4] At the top of the list is the Fourth District in Chiba with 266,071 eligible voters per representative in the lower house, and at the bottom of the list is the Fifth District in Hyogo with 80,249 voters. This ranked list of districts was divided in two using the national average as the cutoff point, thus making two lists, one for underrepresented districts and the other for overrepresented districts. The two lists were then subdivided into two groups, providing four groups of districts, which we will call A, B, C, and D, going from the most underrepresented to the most overrepresented.

Representation		Number of Districts	Number of Representatives
Underrepresented	A	25	95
	B	26	103
	Subtotals	51	198
. . . .			
Overrepresented:	C	38	153
	D	41	160
	Subtotals	79	313

Obviously, there are more overrepresented districts and more legislators from such districts. Included in group A, the most underrepresented, are five districts in Tokyo, four in Osaka, and a number of districts in prefectures surrounding these two cities, such as Chiba, Saitama, and Kanagawa around Tokyo, and Hyogo and Kyoto near Osaka, plus a few regional cities. Districts in group A, then, are those that in recent years have experienced tremendous population growth, mostly by migration.

It is interesting to see how Liberal Democratic candidates running in these four groups fared in the December 1976 national election. The following percentages of LDP candidates were elected:

A: 34.7 (33 out of 95)
B: 44.4 (45 out of 103)
C: 49.0 (75 out of 153)
D: 60.0 (96 out of 160)

The data clearly show how much the Liberal Democratic party depends on the less-populated areas. Just under 35 percent of its candidates were returned from the most populated districts, but 60 percent were returned from the forty-one least populated districts. As one proceeds from group A to D, the Liberal Democratic percentage of elected legislators gets larger step by step. There are obviously more Liberal Democratic legislators from the rural areas than from the big cities, and therefore the party as a whole is probably more sensitive to rural needs and demands than to needs and demands coming from the urban sections of the nation.

Another bit of evidence reinforces the argument that the major source of LDP support is overrepresented rural areas. After the December 1976 election, the newspaper *Sankei* published a list of the Liberal Democratic party faction leaders.[5] All but one had been elected from districts in the D category, that is, the most overrepresented districts. The faction leaders, their districts, and their categories are as follows:

Fukuda (Gumma 3)   D
Tanaka (Niigata 3)   D
Ohira (Kagawa 2)   D
Shiina (Iwate 2)   D
Mizuta (Chiba 3)   D
Funada (Tochigi 1)   C
Miki (Tokushima)   D
Nakasone (Gumma 3)   D

Privatization

The prosperity of the 1960s has also been associated with a general decline in electoral turnout. The percentage of eligible voters who take the trouble to go to the polling booth and cast their ballots varies, of course, from election to election. The level of the election, whether national or local, and the region, whether rural or urban, influences the turnout. Generally speaking, more people vote in local elections than in national elections, and a higher proportion of eligible voters cast ballots in rural precincts than in precincts in large cities. In recent years, the decline in voting

Table 5-4

Youth and Intention to Vote, 1953-1968

Age groups	1953	1963	1968
20-24	54%	39%	34%
25-29	59	47	40
Average for all ages	62	53	51

Source :   Tokeisuri Kenkyujo.   Dai-2 Nihonjin no Kokuminsei, p. 475.

has been particularly conspicuous in the metropolitan areas.

Age is also a factor here. By and large, those in their middle years are most active, and the young and old are less inclined to take the trouble to vote. But in recent years, the drop in the voting rate among youth has been particularly noticeable. This is clearly shown in the longitudinal surveys carried out by the Institute of Mathematical Statistics at five-year intervals since 1953. Table 5-4 shows the intention to vote on the part of youth. As the table shows, between 1953 and 1968 the average percentage for all ages of those intending to vote fell 11 percentage points, but during the same time span, the decline was 20 percentage points for those between twenty and twenty-four years of age. This tendency is confirmed by other data. For instance, election commissions, which are interested in achieving a high turnout, have carried out surveys to find out what groups are not voting. According to their estimates, in 1952 about 15 percent of youth in their twenties abstained from voting in the House of Representatives elections, but by 1969 about 29 percent abstained.[6]

One reason for not voting is probably the change brought about in social networks, particularly on the part of young men and women who have migrated from the rural areas to the cities. Another reason (and this would appear to apply more to those who were born and raised in the cities, although it could also affect migrants) is privatization.

Maruyama Masao has argued that modernization leads to "individuation," by which he means that persons who once lived in "traditional" society become emancipated from the "communal" ties that bound them and prescribed certain traditional behavior.[7] Robert J. Lifton interviewed a small sample of Japanese youth and found them concerned with the idea of *shutaisei,* or selfhood. They had a great desire to have and live by personal convictions and to join with like-minded individuals to achieve goals, that is, to have social commitment. Lifton went on to say that their difficulty "is in realizing to their own satisfaction its first element, that of selfhood; and the sense of 'smallness' or the 'inferiority complex' which they talk so much about seems to reflect the great difficulty the Japanese have in perceiving and believing in a relatively independent self."[8] That youth should want to break out of their sense of dependency, which, as we have seen, is a basic personality trait among Japanese, is not altogether strange.

It appears that young people increasingly seek to achieve selfhood. One of the questions in the national character survey of the Institute of Mathematical Statistics had to do with "goals in life," and among the choices offered respondents was "Don't think about money or fame; just lead a life that suits your own tastes." In 1953, 34 percent of those between twenty and twenty-four years old chose this particular goal, but by 1968 the percentage had risen to 51 percent in this age bracket. The shift, moreover, seems to represent intergenerational change, that is, the characteristic is more pronounced among those born more recently.[9] Thus, what Maruyama has called the trend toward individuation is unmistakably present.

There are four ways, according to Maruyama, in which individuation proceeds. One of these is privatization. The privatized individual is "oriented towards the achievement of self-gratification rather than public goals," does not take the initiative in associating with neighbors, and withdraws from politics as a conscious "reaction against the increasing bureaucratization of the system and against the complexities of the social and political process in which he finds himself involved."[10]

There is indeed evidence that youth are oriented toward self-gratification and away from public goals. Before the war, the Japanese educational system, as well as official government propaganda, stressed the obligation of each individual to put family, society, and the state above himself or herself. The state was likened to a large family with the emperor as the patriarchal father. It was the duty of all subjects, as filial children, to be prepared to sacrifice personal goals, ambitions, and welfare for the good of the whole. The older generation—born and educated before the war—still retain vestiges of this training.

By contrast, young people who were socialized in a more democratic milieu and educational system have a different outlook. The result is a generation gap. Youth put the highest priority on their own welfare and on the gratification of personal wants and goals. The prosperity of the 1960s, moreover, provided most of them with the wherewithal to indulge in self-gratification. A booming economy led to an acute labor shortage, and unemployment virtually disappeared. In many cases, students in the leading universities were signed up by prospective employers by the time they were juniors.

One of the questions in the 1968 national character survey sought to probe the relationship between individual rights and public interest. It read: "There are the following opinions, which do you approve? Of course, it may depend on the situation and degree, but in general which one should be followed? (a) in order to give recognition to one's rights, it may sometimes be necessary to sacrifice the public interest; (b) an individual's rights may sometimes have to be sacrificed in order to promote the public interest."

The responses are given in table 5-5. The data seem to be consistent with the privatization theory. Generally, the younger age groups stress individual rights more than the older generation does. If one compares those between twenty and twenty-four years old with those between fifty and fifty-four years old, there is a difference of seventeen percentage points. One might conjecture that young people, who tend to be more idealistic, overwhelmingly favor putting the public interest above individual rights, but this does not seem to be the case.

Prosperity, Inflation, and Pollution

It may be stated as a truism that when politicians go about trying to solve problems, they invariably end up creating new ones. The Japanese experience with prosperity is a case in point. The economic growth of the 1960s was in part a direct consequence of government policy. The policy was originally associated with the late Prime Minister Ikeda Hayato and was initiated in response to the political situation, which was characterized by confrontations between the ruling party and the Left opposition. The climax in confrontation politics was reached in 1960, when the Left mounted large-scale demonstrations to protest the signing of the revised mutual security treaty with the United States. As a consequence of the demonstrations, the conservative Prime Minister Kishi Nobusuke was forced to resign. Ikeda, his successor, a career bureaucrat and tax specialist, adopted the "low posture" stance of deliberately avoiding policies that

Table 5-5

Age and Individual Rights
vs. Public Interest, 1968

Age group	Individual rights	Public interest	Other	N
20-24	46%	50%	4%	376
25-29	38	52	10	398
30-34	42	48	10	399
35-39	32	59	9	389
40-44	28	66	6	344
45-49	33	58	9	243
50-54	29	60	11	222
55-59	26	60	14	205
60-	19	62	19	457
Average	33	57	10	

Source: Tokeisuri Kenkyujo, <u>Kokuminsei no Kenkyu</u>, p. 118.

would stir up the opposition forces. He advocated an economic plan designed to double national income within one decade. The plan turned out to be much more successful than even the optimists had envisaged when it was first announced. At the end of the 1960s, Japan's GNP was the third largest in the world, behind that of the United States and the Soviet Union.

But there were costs, the most important being persistent inflation and pollution of the environment.

The prices of commodities and the cost of services rose with persistent regularity during the 1960s, with the trend accelerating after 1965. The trend continued in the 1970s, but at a somewhat slower pace. For many people, income rose at a faster rate than the rise in the cost of living. It should be remembered, however, that there were pernicious side effects from the inflationary spiral. The value of savings and insurance, for example, was steadily eroded by the decline in their purchasing power. Inflation was also particularly harmful to older people whose wages did not rise as rapidly or who were dependent on fixed incomes, such as pensions.

A particularly aggravating problem was the spectacular increase in land values, especially in and near the metropolitan areas. Between 1955 and 1968 land prices rose at least tenfold. In 1977, residential land within easy commuting distance of downtown Tokyo was selling at the equivalent of several million dollars per acre. Construction costs also have skyrocketed, partly because lumber and other materials are mostly imported from abroad. Real estate speculators have no doubt profited, but the average middle-class family has been completely squeezed out of the housing market. Most Japanese dream of owning a small house with a garden, but the dream has become simply unattainable.

The other problem, pollution, like inflation, has become painfully evident to everyone. Air pollution, particularly in the populous industrialized regions, has reached levels where it has begun to affect the health of the inhabitants.

Stories are told of policemen directing traffic who are forced to go into the police station to get whiffs of oxygen. As a publicity stunt, one enterprising department store sent some employees to Mount Fuji to fill empty cans with clean mountain air. These cans of mountain air were then given to the store's customers.

Water pollution, both in rivers and in the seas around Japan, has also reached almost intolerable levels. One would be hard put to find a river of any size in Japan that is clear and sparkling. The paper and chemical industries are especially guilty of blithely dumping poisonous wastes into rivers. There have been cases where people have either died or been crippled from eating fish taken out of rivers polluted with mercury wastes. In some instances, the victims have sought redress in the courts and have won damage suits against firms found guilty of polluting the environment. Unfortunately, even if one does win a damage suit, one's health is not restored.

The problem with both inflation and pollution is that they are beyond the control of individuals. A single individual can do very little about them. Thus, the solution is left basically up to the government.

It is not that the Japanese government has failed to act either against inflation or pollution. From time to time, the monetary authorities have restricted credit to slow down inflation, thereby producing business recessions. With regard to pollution, in recent years a number of antipollution laws have been put on the books, but whether they are comprehensive enough and will be enforced with vigor remains to be seen. Thus, despite government efforts to deal with inflation and pollution, the public at large has not been convinced that those in authority are doing much to get at the heart of these problems. Recent public opinion surveys report that most people continue to be troubled by them.

Because the Liberal Democratic party has been in power continuously since 1955, when it came into existence as a result of a merger of two small conservative parties, it is not surprising that it should be blamed for failure to act more decisively. The party in power can take the credit for prosperity, but it must also bear the onus of having failed to stop inflation and the pollution of the environment—even though that might be unfair, since most governments have been unable to solve these problems adequately.

Changes in Party Support

Given the negative aspects of economic growth described above, it is understandable that criticisms of the LDP-controlled government should become more pronounced with the passage of time. The Japan Broadcasting Corporation, which carried out a public opinion survey on eve of the 1974 House of Councillors election, found that dissatisfaction had risen since the 1972 poll for the House of Representatives election. The results are summarized in table 5-6. As the table shows, in 1972, 60 percent of those who had opinions indicated some degree of dissatisfaction, but in 1974 the figure had risen to 70 percent.

Table 5-6

Attitude Toward the National Government,
1972, 1974

Attitude	1972	1974
Satisfied	5%	3%
Satisfied by and large	28	21
Dissatisfied by and large	47	48
Dissatisfied	13	22

Source: Kohei Shinsaku. "Taisei Sentaku no Seiji Ishiki" (Systemic Choice and Political Attitudes). Bunken Geppo, November 1974, p. 5.

Nevertheless, there is considerable variation in the degree of dissatisfaction. One important variable is party support. In general, those who support the ruling party tend to feel that the party is doing a pretty good job, everything considered, and are wont to point to extenuating circumstances to explain away the party's weaknesses. At the other extreme are the Communists, who are the most critical, followed by the Socialists and supporters of the Clean Government party. Of those who belong to the opposition, followers of the Democratic Socialist party are generally the least critical of the ruling party.[11]

Another variable, which is not totally unrelated to party support, is the urban-rural dimension. The level of dissatisfaction is highest in the large cities, where pollution is more acute, where land costs are unbearably high, and where overcrowding is most visible. It is lowest in the towns and rural districts where the environment remains more benign.

Despite signs of growing dissatisfaction with politics in general and the Liberal Democratic party in particular, there seems to be no overwhelming desire to put the Liberal Democrats out of power. In the same 1974 survey, the Japanese Broadcasting Corporation asked 2,647 respondents about the long-run future of Japanese politics in terms of what party should rule. Table 5-7 summarizes the results. Only about one-fourth of those interviewed wanted to see a transfer of power to one or more of the opposition parties. The Japanese people are apparently not willing, at least now, to support a fairly drastic form of political change.

This is borne out by the rate of shifts from one political party to another, or from a party to "no party" preference. There is no evidence that dissatisfaction with the Liberal Democratic party has resulted in a massive desertion of the party. According to a survey conducted during the 1971 House of Councillors' election, about 17 percent of those who reported some kind of party affiliation had changed

Table 5-7

Who Should Govern in the Future?

Want the LDP regime to stay in power	24%
Can't be helped if the LDP stays in power	34
Want the opposition to take over	25
100% = 2,647	

Source: Kohei Shinsaku. "Taisei Sentaku no Seiji Ishiki," p. 20.

parties during the last few years. The Clean Government party had the lowest desertion rate, followed by the Liberal Democratic party. The Democratic Socialist and Communist parties (in that order) had higher desertion rates than the Liberal Democrats. Liberal Democratic deserters went to all parties, but the Democratic Socialist party absorbed more of them than the other parties did. As might be expected, Socialist party deserters went to the Democratic Socialist and Communist parties. Interestingly enough, the percentage of those shifting parties was lower in Tokyo than in other large cities (7.3. percent vs. 12.8 percent). This is probably related to the fact that Tokyo has a higher proportion of those who belong to the young and old generations, and of those with low incomes.[12]

A phenomenon that may have even more long-range significance than shifts from one party to another is the growing proportion of the electorate with no party preference. There have always been a certain number of people who are for one reason or another indifferent to politics. They are simply not interested in politics, pay little attention to it, have no opinion one way or another about it, and hence do not identify with any political party. But those who have "no party" are somewhat different. They may be interested in politics, have definite views about it, and may take the trouble to keep themselves informed about what is happening in the political world. But they refuse to commit themselves to a particular political party. They may feel that no existing party meets their ideal of what a party should be; they may reject the parliamentary system and favor instead some form of direct participatory democracy; or they may prefer to seek out candidates whose career backgrounds, personal qualities, and ideological positions they like regardless of the candidate's party affiliation.

According to recent survey data, about 40 percent of those interviewed say they do not support any political party. A relatively small percentage of these individuals are indifferent to politics. Most of them fall into the second category of no party preference.

The "no party" phenomenon has no geographical basis; it is essentially national in character and cuts across urban-rural and regional divisions. But it does appear to be somewhat related to age, as indicated in table 5-8. Compared to people in their prime, that is, in their forties, the younger

Table 5-8

Age and Commitment to Party, 1971

Age	Support one of five parties	"No party," "Don't know"	Have changed parties
20-29	48.4%	51.6%	11.9%
30-39	60.8	39.2	11.6
40-49	64.6	35.4	11.4
50-59	57.5	42.5	6.0
60-	59.2	40.8	7.7

Source: Nakamura Kei-ichi. "Datsu Seito-ka Gensho ni tsuite" (On the No-party Phenomenon). Senkyo 25 (August 1972), p. 15.

generation is much less committed to one of the established parties. This fact is undoubtedly related to the decline of traditional values, changing social networks, and privatization discussed earlier. It may be that as younger people get older and acquire a stake in the established order, they begin to develop a sense of loyalty to one party or another. In any case, the decline in commitment to a particular party suggests that the stability and incremental change that have characterized Japanese politics may not endure. There is already some indication that political issues came to play a more important role in national elections during the 1960s and 1970s than they had previously.[13] A period characterized by more volatility and rapid shifts in party fortunes appears to lay ahead.

6
The Minobe Phenomenon

An important development in urban politics in recent years is the growing strength displayed by left-wing forces in a period of rising prosperity. Conservative mayors and governors have been ousted by radical contenders in a number of urban and metropolitan districts. The election of Minobe Ryokichi as governor of Tokyo in 1967, which was part of this trend, commanded widespread attention because of the size and importance of the great city of Tokyo, the nation's capital.

In this election, a little more than two out of three eligible voters actually went to the polls. The turnout was somewhat lower than in the 1959 election, when 70.11 percent voted, but was almost unchanged from the previous election held in 1963. Minobe, a Marxist economics professor, was one of ten candidates. He ran nominally as an independent, but it was widely known that he had the active support of both the Socialist and Communist parties. He failed to get a majority and had to be satisfied with 44.5 percent of the vote. His only serious opponent was Matsushita Masatoshi, a lawyer, who had the backing of both the Liberal Democratic and Democratic Socialist parties. Matsushita was not far behind with 41.7 percent. A third candidate, Abe Kenichi, supported by the Clean Government party, ran a poor third, with only

12.2 percent of the vote. The remaining seven candidates together secured only 1.6 percent.

The Minobe name was not entirely unknown, a factor that may have worked in his favor. His father, Minobe Tatsukichi, also a professor and an eminent authority on the constitution, had been persecuted in the mid-1930s for his doctrine of the emperor as an "organ" of the state, a theory that offended the militarists. Another factor that may also have helped Minobe was his exposure on television. He had appeared earlier on a series of programs on economics, which is said to have attracted a wide audience, especially among housewives.

After having served one term as the first left-wing governor of Tokyo, Minobe decided to run for reelection in 1971. The Liberal Democrats, who were obviously not happy to see a leftist hold the job of chief executive of the capital and largest and most important city in the nation, put in Hatano Akira to run against him. Hatano was relatively well known to Tokyo residents because he had served as the director general of the Metropolitan Police Department. The Liberal Democrats apparently did not go all out to support him, however, because they were aware that their party was not particularly popular with Tokyoites. But they did pledge to give Hatano a huge subsidy of more than $11 billion for the further development of the city of Tokyo. But the prospect of more money for development did not sit well with most residents, who were already suffering from excessive pollution, noise, and overcrowding. They were definitely not in favor of more development. Moreover, development was associated with the central government, and they wanted less interference by the government and more autonomy for the Tokyo municipal authorities.

The two contenders campaigned hard and managed to stir up a good deal of interest among the inhabitants of the city, with the result that more than 72 percent of the eligible voters went to the polls, the highest figure of any election in this big city. The outcome was an overwhelming victory for Minobe, who got a little more than 3.6 million votes to Hatano's 1.9 million, or a 65 to 35 margin. At the same time, Minobe set an all-time record for the number of votes cast for a single candidate.

The results of the election are, of course, subject to a variety of interpretations. The left wing, for instance, could argue that the election represented a victory for its cause and could claim that it was a prelude to other favorable outcomes at other levels of government. Nevertheless, the Left did not do nearly so well in elections for mayors and city councilmen held at the same time in the various cities that make up the Greater Tokyo area. For example, only one out of the eight contested mayorships was won by a left-wing candidate.

Conservatives, by contrast, could find solace in the view that Minobe's impressive showing resulted from his personality and public image rather than from his ideology or policies.[1] There is no doubt that Minobe enjoyed widespread popularity, but he also had the support of more than 90 percent of Socialist and Communist voters.[2]

Another view, put forward by Taketsugu Tsurutani, is that the Minobe victory represents "a new political orientation and a new pattern of political awareness and participation." He argues that "voters no longer view periodic elections conducted by political parties as capable of bringing about the changes required in a fast-changing society. They are seeking, instead, to bring about such change themselves through a new way of political action."[3] The new way, according to Tsurutani, is the formation of citizens' organizations, which had worked for Minobe's reelection. "It was indeed the first time in Japan's electoral history that many ordinary citizens participated effectively in the political process in such a direct and immediate fashion. As some commentators noted, the Minobe victory was the expression of 'citizen power'."[4]

Although this is a plausible theory, Tsurutani unfortunately does not provide evidence of a *direct* causal relationship between "citizen power" and the electoral outcome. He simply notes that some citizens' organizations worked for Minobe (but some also worked for Hatano) and assumes that they propelled Minobe into the governorship for the second term. A closer look at the election may explain the outcome more adequately.

Shifting Party Loyalties

In a parliamentary system, the electorate does not have an opportunity to indicate its preference for the chief executive, at least directly, as it does in a presidential system. However, some say that in Great Britain general elections "are fought to a large extent, between two rival candidates for the Prime Ministership."[5] That is, when the average voter supports a particular MP, he feels that he is also backing the Tory or Labour leader who will become the next prime minister. This does not seem to be the case in Japan, although there are no reliable data on this point. For one thing, since there is no two-party arrangement in Japan, there is no possibility of a contest between two rival prime ministers.

Japanese voters, however, can help choose chief executives at the prefectural and municipal levels, that is, governors and mayors. In both instances, it seems, citizens often approach the matter in a somewhat different way than when casting ballots for a member of the National Diet. In a national election, party affiliation can be expected to exert a stronger pull for several reasons. First of all, it is harder to make judgments about the past political performance of a national legislator. He is only one of several hundred legislators who collectively help determine public policies. This is all the more so in systems, like the one that prevails in Japan, where party discipline is imposed on voting for legislative bills. In prefectural and mayoral elections, by contrast, the public has a better opportunity to make some judgment about the ability and performance of a governor or a mayor. Second, the voters have probably figured out that an independent is virtually helpless in a legislature where action takes place along party lines. A legislator must necessarily be a member of a political party, preferably a party in power, if he or she is to bring any influence to bear on what goes on. But a governor or mayor, being a chief executive, need not be a party member to be effective.

Perhaps this explains why, at least in Tokyo, voters show different degrees of party loyalty depending on the level at which the election takes place. Specifically, we are interested in attitudes that prevail during an election for the governor of Tokyo. The results of a survey on party support conducted before the 1971 election are shown in table 6-1. Two com-

Table 6-1

Party Support for House of Representatives and
Tokyo Governorship Elections, 1971

Party	House of Representatives	Governor of Tokyo
Liberal Democratic	36.2%	23.7%
Socialist	16.9	20.4
Democratic Socialist	7.9	2.5
Clean Government	4.4	3.3
Communist	6.3	5.8
Support no party	19.3	31.3
Don't know; other	9.0	13.0

Source: Okubo Sadayoshi. "Tomin no Tohyo Kodo to Seiji Ishiki" (Political Consciousness and Voting Behavior of Tokyo Residents), Senkyo 24 (April 1971), p. 25.

ments can be made about the data in table 6-1. First, a much lower proportion of Liberal Democrats voted for the LDP candidate for governor than voted for LDP candidates for the House of Representatives. The second feature, which is related to the first, is that the proportion of those who profess to support no party at all rose sharply in the election for the governorship. In other words, except for the Socialist party, all parties lost supporters at the governorship level.

One possible explanation for the decline of partisanship is that the electorate regards the personal qualifications of the candidate for governor as more important than his party affiliation. According to a poll conducted by the newspaper *Mainichi*, 69 percent of the respondents said they would vote for a candidate they liked even if the candidate was endorsed by a party or organization that they did not support.[6]

Another explanation for this decline of party support is that the LDP's long monopoly of power at the national level has produced among voters a "feeling of distrust, impotence, of frustration over a condition of party politics where any real likelihood of a change in regime (a major merit of parliamentary democracy) has vanished."[7] As a result, some people become so-called floating voters. Such voters may be opposed to political parties per se, but they are not necessarily opposed to politics per se. Indeed, some observers have argued that Tokyoites voting for Minobe is roughly equivalent to Americans switching from Republicans to Democrats.[8] Because Tokyoites saw no immediate prospect of getting the Liberal Democrats out of the national government, they voted for Minobe at least to get a different kind of regime at the metropolitan level. In any case, there is no question that in the 1971 gubernatorial election, personal qualifications and appeal played an important part.

In terms of personal appeal, Minobe was quite clearly far ahead of his opponent. It is said that the "Minobe smile" appealed particularly to women voters, who now outnumber men in Tokyo. Of the qualities that people admired most in Minobe, perhaps the most positive was "trustworthiness." His supporters perceived him to be a leader who could be trusted.[9] Hatano, on the other hand, projected strength, a befitting image for a former chief of police. In this instance, then, voters apparently tended to prefer someone whom they could trust to someone who could lead them with a strong hand.

It is hard to say in any objective sense that Minobe succeeded in solving important problems during his first administration. His policy was the "defense of the lives of the people of Tokyo," and he did institute a number of reforms. For instance, he stepped up aid to health and education, provided free medical care for the aged, instituted a child allowance system, abolished public gambling, enacted antipollution ordinances, and demanded removal of a U.S. army field hospital located in Tokyo.[10] But he did not make much headway against inflation, pollution of the environment, overcrowding, and inadequate housing; no governor, however able, could singlehandedly have solved these problems. Indeed, even the national government, with resources much greater than those of Tokyo, had not been able to come to grips with these enormous problems. Tokyo voters seemed aware, however, that there were many problems that Minobe could not solve and so did not blame him when he failed to solve them.

In short, Minobe's success was due less to his record of achievement than to his personal style of politics. He ran a rather open administration, he was accessible to the residents of Tokyo, and he indicated his willingness to listen to their complaints. He engaged in a "dialogue" with the inhabitants of the city, and they appreciated it. Such satisfaction with the Minobe administration was an important factor in public support for his reelection, as table 6-2 shows. A little more than six out of ten Minobe supporters expressed satisfaction with his administration. Only about one out of eight was dissatisfied. Among those who supported his opponent, there was a higher percentage of dissatisfied than of satisfied citizens. Even among Hatano supporters, however, more than one-fifth were satisfied with the Minobe regime. Finally, the undecided were about evenly distributed between the satisfied and dissatisfied groups. Thus the satisfaction-dissatisfaction dimension appears to be an important variable in the vote, but party loyalty induced some voters to vote for a candidate despite dissatisfaction.

Table 6-2

Support for Candidates for Governor as Related
to Satisfaction with Minobe Government

Candidate supported	Satisfied	Dissatisfied	Neither	Don't know
Minobe	61.8%	12.2%	19.9%	6.1%
Hatano	22.9	32.5	32.5	12.0
Undecided	26.6	25.0	31.9	16.5

Source: Okubo Sadayoshi.   "Tomin no Tohyo Kodo to Seiji Ishiki."   Senkyo 24 (April 1971), p. 18.

Another factor affecting the vote was the socioeconomic variable. As one might expect, the more affluent groups, particularly those engaged in business, preferred Hatano over the leftist Minobe. Hatano ran more strongly in the inner city districts where there are substantial numbers of independent businessmen, and Minobe got impressive support in the suburban bedroom communities where there are concentrations of commuters, particularly white-collar workers.[11]

The relationship between affluence and preference for Hatano, however, was tempered by the educational variable. In general, people with a higher level of education have better-paying jobs and thus could have been expected to vote for Hatano. But the better educated also tend to be better informed about political affairs, which, in turn, often makes them rather critical of the existing political parties and their policies. In this election, there was a correlation between the level of education and support for Minobe. The higher the educational level, the higher the level of support indicated for the incumbent governor.[12]

Obviously, there was another "pull" operating here, and that was party loyalty. As has been suggested, partisanship along party lines is much weaker at the municipal level, but party loyalty is still a significant factor. According to Shiratori's calculations, about 21.3 percent of his sample of voters said they would vote on the basis of party, 56.7 percent on the basis of their judgment of the candidates' qualifications, 15.6 percent would follow both party and candidate qualifications, and 6.2 percent could not or would not state their preferences.[13] Interestingly enough, those who supported Hatano and those who supported Minobe divided differently along this dimension. Although Minobe enjoyed the strong backing of the Left, more would support him on the basis of his appeal as a candidate than would do so out of party loyalty (59.0 percent vs. 45.4 percent). This can be seen from table 6-3.

Table 6-3

Voter Support for Hatano and Minobe on
the Basis of Party or Candidate

Support for	Voting on the basis of party (21.3% of whole sample)	Voting on the basis of candidate (56.7% of whole sample)	Percent of whole sample
Hatano	34.0%	14.0%	18.1%
Minobe	45.4	59.0	51.8

Source: Shiratori Rei. <u>Seron, Senkyo, Seiji</u>, p. 44.

Among Hatano's backers, party appears to have been a much more important consideration: those with a definite commitment to the Liberal Democratic party outnumbered those who were impressed by his personal qualifications. Hatano's problem was that he was unable to make significant inroads into the no-party group, the largest single category in Tokyo politics.

Minobe got overwhelming support from the Socialist and Communist regulars, who probably accounted for at least half of his 3.6 million votes (in all, 5.5 million votes were cast). Minobe got the other half of his vote from all the other parties, including the Liberal Democratic party, as well as from the "floating" voters. In short, he succeeded in doing what every winning candidate must be able to do, that is, put together a broad coalition based on party loyalty plus personal appeal.[14]

Fluidity in Politics

The Minobe election in 1971 also suggests that an important characteristic of recent Tokyo politics is its fluidity. It is fluid in part because the degree of commitment to the established political parties has been on the decline in recent years. Party loyalty no longer seems to provide much of a guideline for a sizable bloc of voters when it comes to choosing the governor. Instead of looking at party labels, many voters are now weighing the pros and cons of individual candidates, trying to judge their personal qualifications for the position of chief executive and to discern what kinds of public policies the candidates are likely to follow. The growing stress on candidates makes it likely that the electoral turnout, that is, the percentage of eligible voters actually going to the polls, will vary substantially in the future. This stress on candidates may indeed presage a trend toward lower turnouts. Candidate-oriented voters will probably tend to stay home unless there is a particularly attractive candidate or unless some issue arouses an emotional response, for instance, revelations of widespread corruption in government.

One would guess that fluidity is a special characteristic

of big city politics and is rooted in the very nature of urban life. To begin with, many city dwellers, unlike those who live on farms, live in one place and work at another. In a big city such as Tokyo, the breadwinner usually commutes, often long distances, to the office, factory, plant, or store. City dwellers, furthermore, are more mobile than rural folk and change residences more often. The total effect of the separation between place of work and residence and of the higher rate of mobility is to inhibit the development of a sense of loyalty to a particular community. Urban people may complain that the roads are bad or that there are inadequate cultural facilities (e.g., libraries and schools) in their community, but unless they spend a good deal of time there and expect to be permanent residents, they may lack the incentive to apply political pressure for improvements.

In addition, commuters may be part of more than one social network. For instance, a commuter may have close personal relationships with work associates, and he may be influenced by what his coworkers are thinking and advocating. At the same time, he may be part of another social network based on family ties, old friendship ties, and perhaps neighborhood ties, although these last are more likely to be rather weak. But in many instances, these social networks may well fail to provide cues for political action for the simple reason that politics may not be particularly relevant to that group, at least at that time. Under these circumstances, political decisions, such as voting—whether to vote and, if voting, for which candidate—are probably influenced more by individual preferences than by group pressure. Compared to rural dwellers, urban residents can be much more independent in their political behavior. "People who live in cities," according to one account, "generally are not bound by ties to locality and by kinship ties. It is said that they make political decisions not on the basis of any special political views but by analyzing, in terms of their own self-interest, their varied needs that emerge from life in the city."[15]

There is very little direct evidence that citizens' groups significantly influenced Tokyo residents to support Minobe, as has been suggested by Tsurutani. Although so-called citizens' groups and residents' groups have proliferated in recent years, according to Shinohara Hajime, the number of persons involved in them appears to be rather small in proportion to the population. On the other hand, Shinohara notes, the number of people who indicate an interest in joining citizens' groups, if such groups were started in their neighborhoods, is much larger. According to one survey, almost 42 percent of the respondents indicated such interest, and a little more than 29 percent said that they would not participate.[16] In a poll undertaken by the Japan Broadcasting Corporation in 1973, 60 percent of the respondents indicated that they had not taken part in political activities other than voting. The other 40 percent had done so, however, and the kinds of activities reported are interesting: 24 percent had signed petitions; 14 percent had contributed money for political purposes; 13 percent had attended political rallies; 11 percent had read publications issued by parties and other political organizations; 5 percent had taken part in protest or lobbying activities; 4 percent had joined in demonstrations; 3 percent had acted as party workers; and finally 1 percent had written letters to the mass media.[17] In general, the number of individuals who took an active part in the political process—protested, lobbied, demonstrated, or worked for a political party—is remarkably small in comparison to the number of eligible voters. In this regard, Japan seems to be no different from other democracies.

In any case, if there were a connection between citizens' movements and support for Minobe, it would stem from Minobe's success in eliciting a positive response from those who were alienated from the established political parties, i.e., from the types who are likely to join citizens' groups.[18]

Dual Polity

A tentative conclusion that may be drawn from the Minobe phenomenon is that something resembling a "dual polity" appears to be emerging in Japan. By dual polity, we mean that what happens politically at the local level is becoming less and less related to what goes on at the national level. This is partly because more and more people seem to make a distinction between these two levels of political activity. It appears that this development is related to the following phenomena.

1. So long as the Japanese were interested in economic growth, they looked to the central government for guidance and assistance, particularly to increase the flow of financial resources from the central treasury to the local communities. Conservative politicians urged voters to support them because they could use their personal connections with the ruling party to get grants and other forms of aid from the central government. Now, except in very poor communities, the prospect of getting more government money for economic development is less attractive than before: the trade-off is more pollution, inflation, overcrowding, and general deterioration in the quality of life.

2. More and more citizens are coming to feel that the central government is becoming less responsive to the needs and demands of the general public. These same people believe that of the two levels—central and local—the local government is more likely to be concerned about the welfare of the people, especially when it comes to taking care of the everyday needs of the public. In this connection, Joseph A. Massey, in a recent study of the image of political leaders among Japanese youth, reports the following exchange with a teenager:

I. So things that are right around you don't seem like politics? If that's the case, whom do you think of when I ask about politicians?

R. The prime minister.

I. What about Governor Minobe?

R. He and some others have been on television a lot recently, making a fuss. . . . In a way, he's a politician, too.

I. But he's different from the prime minister?

R. Yes, more like the working people.

I. What do you mean by that? He feels closer to you?

R. The things he does are basic, [sort of between doing] things for the country and for one's home.

I. Things like garbage collection don't seem like politics?

R. No.[19]

Massey then goes on to comment that the teenage respondent was hesitant about calling Governor Minobe a politician and that the interviewer, who happened to be a Japanese college girl, "provides us with the clue to the image of the local leader's job: not politics but 'things like garbage collection'." According to this view, local autonomy is "local officials looking after the practical needs of the common citizens."[20]

For many people, then, "politics" is something that goes on far away and is rather remote from their personal life. It is not surprising, therefore, that most Japanese do not have much affect for their national political leaders. But, as Massey suggests, they see local leaders such as mayors and village chiefs in a somewhat different light—as benevolent, paternalistic leaders who look after the welfare of their followers. That role is consonant with the feelings of dependency that are characteristic of Japanese psychological makeup, the importance that Japanese attach to their relations with others in small groups, and their concept of the responsibilities of leaders. Those who adopt a no-party stance at the local level are probably particularly likely to see mayors and other local leaders as patrons rather than as politicians. What goes on at this level is not "politics," hence there is no place for partisanship.

If a "dual polity" is a characteristic of Japanese politics, then Governor Minobe's victory is not necessarily a "leading indicator" of an eventual left-wing victory at the national level. Minobe's showing in 1971 represented a fairly complex phenomenon, one that cannot be characterized simply as a Socialist-Communist triumph at the polls.

Postscript on Minobe

As Minobe's second term as governor of Tokyo approached its end in 1975, he announced, after some hesitation, that he would run for a third term. Like many other governors, Minobe discovered that he was subject to third-term losses. In general, governors tend to do well when they try for the second term, but they often fail to win the same number of votes on the third time around.

The Liberal Democratic party put up Ishihara Shintaro, a popular and well-known novelist-turned politician. (He actually ran as an independent.) Minobe enjoyed the backing of the Socialist, Communist, and Clean Government parties. The Democratic Socialists supported Matsushita Masatoshi, who had run unsuccessfully against Minobe in 1967 and who was a member of the House of Councillors, thereby making it a three-way race. The results of the election were as follows:

Minobe	50.5%
Ishihara	43.9
Matsushita	5.1

Minobe won, but compared to the previous election, his share of the vote dropped sharply: from 65 percent to a little more than 50 percent. There was clearly much less enthusiasm for Minobe, and this was reflected in the turnout. In 1971, 72 percent of those eligible voted; this dropped to 67 percent in 1975.

The lower level of interest may have been caused, in part,

by the lack of controversial issues. One of Minobe's accomplishments was an increase in the number of social welfare programs for Tokyo residents. This no doubt won him support, but at the same time the cost of such programs, together with the general expansion of the city government and rising costs in general, produced large municipal deficits, a fact that must have troubled some people. A Liberal Democratic governor would presumably be in a better position to secure financial assistance from the central government than the left-leaning Minobe, but it appears that many Tokyoites were not particularly pleased with the prospect of giving up some local autonomy in return for help from the central government. In any case, the question of social welfare programs versus deficits does not seem to have stirred up Tokyo voters.

Another feature of the 1975 election was an increase in the number of voters who viewed themselves as belonging to the "no party" group. Shiratori's survey of Tokyo voters in 1971 put 27.2 percent of the respondents in this category. By contrast, the Tokyo Election Commission's poll shortly after the 1975 race for the governorship registered 53.6 percent in the "no party" category. Incidentally, the same commission took an earlier poll in 1974 immediately after the House of Councillors election and put the size of the "no party" group at 25.7 percent, which indicates that Tokyo voters approach national and local elections somewhat differently.[21]

Hashimoto Akikazu's estimate of the "no party" group is somewhat higher, a little over 60 percent, and he believes that voters in this category divided as follows: for every four for Minobe, there were three for Ishihara and one for Matsushita.[22] Hashimoto also suggests that of the roughly 40 percent of the voters who indicated support for one party or another, probably 80 to 90 percent voted along party lines, that is, the Liberal Democrats for Ishihara, and the Communists, Socialists, and Clean Government party members for Minobe. Matsushita, the Democratic Socialist candidate (like the others, officially nonpartisan) seems to have obtained only about one half of the Democratic Socialist support.[23]

In general, Minobe won the backing of those who were dissatisfied with prevailing conditions and wanted to see some changes instituted. Over the years, Tokyo residents have been concerned about such matters as pollution, housing, inflation, public facilities (e.g., parks), and social welfare.[24] Minobe had done something about social welfare, but even in this area there were limits to the capability of a large city government to deal comprehensively with such a large problem. Obviously, there were severe limitations on Minobe's ability to deal effectively with inflation, pollution, and housing. Perhaps this is the reason that there was much less enthusiasm for him the third time around. When he sought reelection in 1971, he had been in office for four years, and the voters probably wanted to give him more time to carry out his program. Now that he had been given additional time, the voters were in a better position to assess his potential as a reformer. It appears that the general assessment was that he had not done badly, but that he was something less than a howling success.

7
Localism

In a classic study of politics in the American South, the late V. O. Key introduced the idea of the "friends and neighbors" effect. He discovered that candidates battling it out in the Democratic party primaries in Alabama normally rolled up huge majorities in their home counties. He cited numerous examples of this and introduced several rather graphic maps demonstrating the extent and persistence of this phenomenon. He described, among others, the case of "Big Jim" Folsom, who ran for governor. Folsom was born in Coffee County in southeastern Alabama, spent his boyhood there, and eventually married the daughter of a probate judge. Later, he lived in Cullman County, located in the northern part of the state. In the election his two strongest counties turned out to be Coffee and Cullman, the latter giving him a 72 percent majority.[1] Quite clearly Alabama voters took kindly to the hometown boy and turned out in large numbers to support him. It was a case of friends and neighbors demonstrating their affection for him.

Judging from the tenor of his remarks, Key was somewhat disdainful of this phenomenon. He suggested that this manifestation of localism pointed to "an absence of stable, well-organized. state-wide factions of likeminded citizens formed to advocate measures of common concern."[2] He described the situation as one where the local leader "gains support, not primarily for what he stands for or because of his capacities, but because of where he lives. A more or less totally irrelevant appeal—back the hometown boy—can exert no little influence over an electorate not habituated to the types of voting behavior characteristic of a two-party situation."[3]

As Key saw it, politics ought to be concerned with public issues and not be sidetracked by such "irrelevant" matters as supporting the hometown boy. "In well-developed two-party situations," he said, "localism is minimized, if not erased, by a larger concern for party victory."[4] Thus, according to Key's vision of democratic politics, political parties should take enduring positions along some ideological dimension, and voters should consistently support one party or another on the basis of their preference for these ideological positions. Thus he explicitly compared Alabama counties to Dutchess County in New York State, home of Franklin Roosevelt. "The county," he wrote, "traditionally Republican, stubbornly held to its partisan attachments and repeatedly failed to return a majority for even its most distinguished son."[5] It seems clear, in this case, that Roosevelt's wealthy neighbors could not stomach his liberal New Deal measures and so voted against him, even though he was a neighbor.

However, Key did admit that voting for the hometown boy "may be rationalized as a calculated promotion of local interest."[6] But he obviously thought that the promotion of local interest was less important than policy issues. Localism does become more understandable, however, if one adopts the patron-client model of democracy. As noted in earlier chapters, in rural areas in Japan there is a desire to increase material well-being by bringing in outside resources and to increase access to the political system by using patron-client networks. In such a situation, it is perfectly rational to support the hometown boy: other things being equal, he is more likely to be helpful in this regard than a candidate from another community. It seems quite conceivable that an analogous situation prevailed in Alabama.

In any case, given what we know about Japanese politics, one would expect to find the friends-and-neighbors effect in Japan. Indeed, it is not difficult to turn up illustrative cases. A typical one is from Shimane prefecture, but it would not be difficult to find other instances.[7]

In the 1967 election held in Shimane for the House of Representatives, seven candidates competed for the four seats at stake. Four of the seven were endorsed by the Liberal Democratic party, two by the Socialists, and one by the Communist party. As indicated in table 7-1, the friends-and-neighbors effect is quite noticeable. Three out of four Liberal Democrats and one out of two Socialists got a higher percentage of the vote in their respective home cities or counties than any outsider did.

Table 7-1

Votes for Four Residents vs. Outsiders
in 1967 House of Representatives
Election, Shimane Prefecture

Candidate	Party	Home city, county	% of home city, county vote for local boy	% Vote in prefecture	% Vote to outsider with highest vote
Hosoda	LDP	Matsue	27.8%	17.2%	20.8%
Takahashi	LDP	Iishi	51.3	17.3	21.0
Ohashi	LDP	Nita	30.4	15.1	26.2
Urabe	Soc.	Ohara	28.5	14.2	24.7

Source: Shimane-ken Senkyo Iinkai. <u>Senkyo no Kiroku</u>
(Election Returns). 1967.

The other Socialist, Godo Shimao, led in eight cities and counties, which would suggest that he relied mostly on organizational votes, that is, support mobilized on his behalf by the unions. Although he did not lead in his home county, he did come in first in his hometown. The fourth Liberal Democratic candidate, Sakurauchi Yoshio, resided in the city of Matsue, which he lost to his fellow Liberal Democrat, but he did win second place in that city with 20.8 percent of the vote. Finally, the Communist candidate, Wada Kazuo, did not lead in any city or county, which is not surprising, given the conservative character of Shimane politics.

Another example of the friends-and-neighbors effect is taken from Jack Lewis's pioneering study of Mishima, a city in Shizuoka prefecture. Several years ago, Mishima won attention because it was one of the few cities in which a conservative-progressive coalition elected a mayor. A split occurred within the Liberal Democratic party organization there, and one of the dissident factions was able to form a coalition with the Left to elect its leader to the office of the mayor.

Among the phenomena that Lewis investigated in his study of Mishima politics was the pull of localism. He found that in the 1971 election for the city assembly, those whom he interviewed tended to support candidates who lived in the same section of town. His respondents were members of the Association to Build a Brighter Mishima, which included both conservatives and progressives. Table 7-2 shows the relationship between the respondent's place of residence and the residence of the candidate he supported in the election.

Twenty-five out of forty-one, or 61 percent of the sample, supported candidates from their own residential areas regardless of the candidate's party affiliation. There was a somewhat stronger tendency for conservatives to back candidates running from their residential districts. "For the conservatives in the three outlying farming districts, the pull of 'localism' seems very strong, as expected. Each of the fourteen conservatives living in Kitaue, Nishikida, and Nakazato supported a candidate from his district."[8] According to the data in table 7-2, nine out of seventeen, or 53 percent, of the leftist respondents supported candidates

Table 7-2

Localism in Mishima Assembly Support
Patterns, 1971

	Conservatives					
			Respondent's residence			
Home of candidate	West Mishima	Central Mishima	East Mishima	Kitaue	Nishikida	Naka-zato
West Mishima	1					
Central Mishima						
East Mishima			1			1
Kitaue		1		2	1	1
Nishikida		3	1		5	
Nakazato						7
Total	1	4	2	2	6	9

	Progressives					
West Mishima						
Central Mishima	1	3	2			
East Mishima						
Kitaue	2					
Nishikida					2	
Nakazato			2			4
Total	4	3	4		2	4

Source: Jack Lewis. Hokaku Rengo: The Politics of Conservative Cooperation in a Japanese City. Ph.D. Dissertation in Political Science, Stanford University, 1974, p. 155.

from their home areas, a somewhat lower percentage than among conservative respondents. Obviously, one case is not enough to decide whether the difference between the conservatives and the Left is accidental or is rooted in ideology. Conceivably, localism could be more characteristic of conservative ideology and political organization, but neither would one expect it to be absent among adherents of the Left in Japan, given the cultural propensity toward small groups and psychological dependency. In fact, J. A. A. Stockwin has written that the Democratic Socialist party was "strong in Osaka, in part, because Nishio, the party chairman, was popular and had a large personal following in that city."[9]

Actually, James Coleman's study of the friends-and-neighbors effect in the printers' unions suggests that at least two factors may be at work, namely, a personal relationship to the candidate and some kind of "local pride." Coleman, noting Key's data on friends-and-neighbors voting, associated it with rural and small-town areas, "for it is in these small communities that voters are more likely to know the candidate personally or to know someone who knows him."[10] He reasons, therefore, that "friends-and-neighbors voting might decrease sharply as the size of the in-group increased. That is, in a large group, mere size makes it less likely that the average voter in the group will vote on the basis of a personal relationship to the candidate."[11] To test his hypothesis, Coleman took data on voting within shops in the printers' union, both in local elections and in international elections. The shops and locals varied in size from three-man and ten-man shops to locals with as many as 9,000 members. He found that the smaller the shop, the greater the tendency to vote for shop mates, that is, the friends-and-neighbors effect. But he also found that, contrary to expectation, when the size of the local got to be 500 or more, the excess vote resulting from the friends-and-neighbors effect did not go down as expected but always remained above 20 percent. Coleman explained this deviation from what was expected in terms of group identification. In a small group, people know the candidate personally, but in larger groups, where this was unlikely, there was the element of local pride. "That is, if friends-and-neighbors voting was simply due to a kind of 'local pride' or group identification, apart from any personal relationship to the candidate, then there would be no reason to expect it to decrease with the size of the shop or local."[12]

In a recently published essay, Tomita Nobuo includes local pride as one of the three reasons for localism in Japan. The other two have been suggested in previous chapters, namely, benefits to the community by bringing in outside resources, and personal advantage gained through access to politicians, that is, help in getting jobs, assistance in dealing with government agencies, and so on. As an example of local pride, Tomita cites the rivalry between two prominent Liberal Democratic politicians, Nakasone Yasuhiro and Fukuda Takeo, both of whom represent the third election district in Gumma prefecture. According to Tomita, Fukuda beat out Nakasone in 1958 to become the top vote-getter in the district and maintained that position until 1969, when Nakasone took top honors. Nakasone worked hard to achieve this victory because he felt that it would enhance his standing as a potential prime minister. In 1972 Fukuda and Tanaka were contenders to succeed Sato Eisaku as prime minister; in the battle, Nakasone backed Tanaka, thereby contributing to Fukuda's defeat. In the election shortly thereafter, the vote for Nakasone dropped markedly, and Fukuda again captured the lead. Tomita suggests that the voters were disappointed that one of the local boys—Fukuda—had not been able to win the prime ministership and blamed it in part on Nakasone.[13] In this instance, local pride had evidently been hurt.

The Tanaka Case

The case of Tanaka Kakuei, a former prime minister and

one of the central figures in the Lockheed scandal that rocked the political world in 1976, is relevant to the investment model proposed in part 1. Tanaka was suspected of having accepted a large bribe from the Lockheed Corporation to facilitate the sale of its planes to the All-Nippon Airways Company. He was indicted on the charge of having violated Japan's foreign exchange laws and subsequently arrested, the first ex–prime minister ever to go to jail. After he spent several weeks in jail, he was released on bail pending trial, which began in January 1977. Because of the charges lodged against him, Tanaka resigned his membership in the Liberal Democratic party but kept his seat in the House of Representatives, which he had held continuously since 1947. He also announced that he would run for reelection in the December 1976 election, this time as an independent.

His district, the Third District in Niigata, one of the northern prefectures, naturally became the focus of national attention; outsiders wondered how Tanaka's constituents would react to his involvement in the Lockheed scandal. The mass media, of course, sent their reporters and cameramen to the Third District and reported the campaign in detail. Tanaka, for his part, campaigned vigorously this time, traveling extensively throughout his district and reportedly meeting 100,000 people, many of whom were members of his support organization (known as the Etsuzankai), which was well organized with branches and activities in numerous communities. According to newspaper accounts, large crowds (over and above those mobilized by his support organization) turned out to hear his campaign speeches and seemingly went away impressed by the image he projected of a forceful leader.[14]

The election results no doubt pleased Tanaka and his followers. Although he ran as an independent with the added disadvantage of the Lockheed scandal, he scored an impressive victory, coming in as the top vote-getter in the Third District. His share of the vote was lower than in the 1972 election, but one must allow for the fact that he was prime minister in 1972 and running in the midst of a Tanaka boom. The 1969 election would probably be more comparable. In 1969 he got 32.9 percent of the vote, so the 36.9 percent he obtained in 1976 is remarkable. Of course, he did well in his hometown. The percentages of the vote he got in his hometown, home county, and the Third District are given below:

Area	*1969*	*1972*	*1976*
Nishiyama (hometown)	73.7	77.1	72.8
Kariba-gun (home county)	61.6	66.4	60.2
Third District	32.9	42.1	36.9

As can be seen, seven out of ten voters in his hometown, and six out of ten in his home county, continued to support him. The Lockheed scandal apparently did not have too much of an effect throughout the entire electoral district.

Generally, his supporters appear to have taken the view that Tanaka had been a loving father to them and that he, like a good father, had worked hard to provide for the welfare of his dependents.

For example, a reporter for the *Asahi* newpaper visited the small mountain community of Sumon, whose support for Tanaka in previous elections had been almost as strong as that of his hometown. Sumon is an economically depressed area where the young leave in large numbers and the suicide rate among the elderly is unusually high. A local leader told the reporter that he would liken Tanaka and the villagers, and even the people of the Third District and the entire prefecture, to a thief and his family. The leader explained that the area, compared to other areas on the Pacific Ocean side of the islands, was poor and dying. Tanaka had saved them from death. This leader then told how Tanaka had used his influence to get the National Railways to put in a through train at a time when local trains that did not make money were being cut back. Similarly, Tanaka had helped to get a highway linking the area to the outside world. Despite all this, he continued, "the nation is making us, Mr. Tanaka, and his supporters in the Third District, look like villains. But to us he is the father who saved us from death. Even if we assume that he took money away from Lockheed to save us—and we can't tell until the court decides—for us, the children, there is no one else, because if the father had not been a thief, we children would have died." The local leader, therefore, felt that the election provided the voters with an opportunity to repay their debt to Tanaka.[15]

In another area, a housewife is also quoted as having said, "We are very much indebted to Mr. Tanaka. So we had the privilege of repaying our debt." But she added, "But how will it turn out next time? We don't know."[16] Does this imply that if Tanaka loses his ability to look after his constituents because of the Lockheed scandal, the voters may turn to someone else?

In summary, the Tanaka case provides a handy illustration of the relationship between the phenomenon of localism and the investment model. Voters, in choosing their representatives, are confronted by information costs and uncertainty. One way to overcome these problems is to support a candidate who is known directly to the voter or indirectly through social networks. As Samuel Popkin et al. put it, "Particularly on distributive issues—which neighborhood to tear up for a highway, where to put the post office, where to distribute patronage—localism may be a very effective operating procedure for the voter to use. At least the voter has some chance of knowing whether or not a neighbor is a blatant crook or an obvious fool."[17] Many of Tanaka's neighbors wanted to secure what we have called divisible benefits, and since he had provided them in the past, they were willing to invest in him again, even though in this particular case there was an indication that he might be a blatant crook. At least he did not steal from them.

8
The Investment Model
and Political Change

The purpose of this chapter is to summarize the main points that have been made about the investment model and to suggest how the model explains some important political changes in Japan during the past twenty years. Much of Japanese politics, at least at the mass level, seems to be chiefly concerned with practical, down-to-earth matters; it displays an unmistakable instrumental quality. This quality, I think, gives Japanese politics, again at the mass level, a more pragmatic than ideological bent.

This same instrumental quality, moreover, makes the investment model particularly appealing in analyzing Japanese politics. The model posits two actors who interact, that is, voters, who may be likened to investors, and politicians, who act as entrepreneurs. Voters, when investing in politicians, basically seek benefits, which may be looked upon as returns on investment. There are at least four kinds of benefits: (1) indivisible, (2) divisible, (3) political party patronage, and (4) individual. Needless to say, preferences for benefits vary depending on individuals, time, and place.

Voters may act politically on the basis of individual choice, but the model also provides for the possibility that voters will be influenced by the social networks in which they are embedded. In the latter case, voter-investors form a kind of consortium and pool their support for particular politicians. There are certain advantages to be gained by adopting this voting strategy. First, information costs can be reduced. Second, the formation of a consortium may often enhance the probability of securing benefits. From the point of view of the democratic system, social networks can also sometimes affect the level and nature of political participation as well as the direction of partisanship.

Politicians, like voters, can also act individually or in groups. A political party may be looked upon as a coalition of politicians. There is an incentive for politicians to form coalitions because the winning coalition can control the government and thereby get access to its vast resources. Obviously, access to resources makes it easier to provide benefits to supporters.

The way in which politicians and voter-investors interact and the distribution of benefits are influenced in part by the institutional framework within which the interaction takes place. Specifically, what we have in mind is the electoral system that converts votes into seats in the House of Representatives. Japan's present electoral system is biased in favor of the less-populous rural districts, resulting in their overrepresentation in the House of Representatives. The ruling party, moreover, is strong in the overrepresented areas, and its faction leaders are also drawn from such areas. The Liberal Democratic party, therefore, is likely to be especially sensitive to the concerns and needs of rural inhabitants, which, it turns out in many cases, can be best met by providing divisible benefits, that is, roads, bridges, schools, in short, public works projects that serve local interests more than national ones.

In addition, the Liberal Democratic party has supported a program of rapid economic growth, which has succeeded in propelling the country into the front ranks of the industrial powers. One consequence of the economic growth of the 1960s and the early 1970s was a massive population shift, especially of young people, from the less-populated sections of the country to the metropolitan areas. The ruling party's style of mobilizing support has not been particularly suited to urban politics for reasons that have been discussed in previous chapters. Furthermore, city dwellers, both long-time residents and newcomers, have often felt that the Liberal Democratic party has not been sufficiently responsive to their needs and concerns. For instance, city dwellers, much more than their rural counterparts, are troubled by inflation, environmental pollution, the prohibitive cost of land and houses, overcrowding, and the inadequacies of existing social security programs. To some extent, the void created by the inability or unwillingness of the two major parties, the Liberal Democratic and the Socialist, to deal effectively with urban problems was filled by the Clean Government and Communist parties, which built up a political following by providing for the daily needs of the population, especially the lower-income and less-privileged sectors. In any case, the net effect of the perceived lack of responsiveness was to turn many voters away from political parties and from national politics.

In terms of the investment model, voters became less willing than before to invest in politicians because the kinds of benefits they sought were not always forthcoming. Many voters shifted their interest toward indivisible benefits, that is, public policies that benefit everyone rather than a limited or localized group of citizens. For example, relief from pollution and inflation can be achieved only through a broadly based national effort.

One way to elaborate on the model, which I have described so far in rather general terms, is to try to apply it to the political developments of the last two decades. Listed below are six significant developments.

1. *Decline in electoral participation.* The largest turnout

of voters occurred in 1958, when 76.99 percent of the national electorate voted. The low point came in 1968, when 68.51 percent turned out. Since then electoral participation has risen somewhat, reaching 73.45 percent in 1976. The decline is not large, but it has occurred in the face of certain developments that seemingly, at least, ought to have stimulated participation. First, the educational level of the nation has been rising steadily. More and more people are staying in school longer. Second, the mass media, particularly television, have grown tremendously, so much so that it would be difficult to find a family that does not have a radio or television set. Third, general income levels have risen, so that people are better off than before in terms of access to material goods. Logically, one would expect all three factors to be conducive to higher rates of political participation, either because they reduce information costs or because they give individuals a stronger sense of political efficacy. (Higher income levels are associated with more participation.)

2. *Decline in the share of the vote obtained by the two major parties.* If we take the total number of votes obtained by the Liberal Democratic party and the Socialist party and divide that figure by the total number of eligible voters (as opposed to those actually voting), we find that the ratio has steadily declined over the years. In 1958, for instance, the combined Liberal Democratic and Socialist vote came to 69.35 percent of the total number of eligible voters. By 1976, it had dropped to 45.37 percent. Since 1969, in other words, the two major parties have failed to win the support of a majority of the electorate.

3. *The rise of urban-based minor parties.* In contrast to the two major parties, the Clean Government party and the Communist party have been getting more and more electoral support. In 1976, for instance, the Clean Government party got 18.2 percent of the vote in Tokyo and 21.4 percent in Osaka, and the Communists got 15.4 percent in Tokyo and 18.9 percent in Osaka. In 1967, by contrast, the Clean

Government party got 13.1 percent and 18.0 percent in Tokyo and Osaka, respectively, and the Communists obtained 9.9 percent in Tokyo and 8.9 percent in Osaka.

4. *Increase in the number of "progressive" mayors and governors.* In recent years, local political units have tended to come under the control of left-leaning political leaders. As we saw in the case of Minobe, enough conservative voters support progressive candidates for local office to enable many of these candidates to win.

5. *Increase in the number of voters who support "no party."* Quite clearly, party identification has been on the decline. It seems that voters are increasingly losing confidence in the established parties.

6. *Increase in the number of so-called citizens' and residents' movements.* This is probably related to the decline in party identification. Those who have lost confidence in established parties often prefer to engage in more direct forms of political participation rather than vote for party politicians.

Some of these developments most certainly must be interrelated. In general voters are apparently less willing to support one or the other of the two major parties on election day and to turn the running of the country over to the party politicians. As the polls indicate, there is a growing dissatisfaction with party politics, especially at the national level. My interpretation is that more and more citizens feel that the major parties are no longer responsive to their needs and concerns and so are turning either to the minor parties or to local political units, such as the prefectural or city governments, to provide the kinds of benefits they seek.

It is my belief that the investment model provides a parsimonious explanation for what has been happening in Japanese politics. People's expectations in the way of benefits have been changing as Japan has become more urban. The Liberal Democratic party and, to a lesser extent, the Socialist party are rural-based and have been unable to respond adequately to the felt needs of urban voters (and recently even of some rural voters). The major parties have not provided the kind of benefits sought. As a result, minor parties have grown, particularly in the urban districts, and alternative forms of participation have been adopted to some extent, especially in the cities. What is clearly needed is a shift toward a mode of politics that is more sensitive to urban concerns.

The system is not completely oblivious to changing voter or investor interests and demands. Because of the steady decline in voter support for the Liberal Democratic party, in the near future the party may no longer be able to monopolize power. Some form of coalition government seems inevitable.

In fact, after the national election of December 1976, the Liberal Democratic party secured enough seats to keep control of the House of Representatives only by enlisting the support of some independents, and there was speculation that the ruling party would very likely suffer defeat in the House of Councillors election set for July 1977. But in this House of Councillors election, the Liberal Democrats again managed to stave off defeat by persuading three successful independent candidates to join the party, thereby obtaining enough seats to maintain a majority.

An analysis of the election results shows that the ruling party continues to suffer decline in popular support. The situation in the House of Councillors is somewhat difficult to interpret because voters choose two candidates, one for the national constituency and another to represent their prefecture. The Liberal Democratic vote in the national constituency, which some consider a rather good indicator of popular sentiment, registered a decline from 44.3 percent in 1974 to 35.8 percent in 1977, a drop of 8.5 percent. In the prefectural contest, however, the Liberal Democratic vote diminished only slightly—from 39.5 percent to 39.46 percent. The ruling party was helped by pro-rural bias built into the electoral system and by the fragmentation of the opposition parties.

In addition to the New Liberal Club, which endorsed candidates in this election (encouraged, no doubt, by its good showing in the House of Representatives election in December 1976), three new minor parties entered the fray. One was the Socialist Citizens' League, a small group led by the late Eda Saburo, a well-known moderate leader, who split off from the Socialist party. Eda died in the spring of 1977, and his son Satsuki, who took over, managed to win election in the national constituency.

Another new minor party was the United Progressive Liberals, composed primarily of people active in the mass media, and the third was a tiny women's liberation group. These four new minor parties, although they elected only five representatives, managed to secure about 10 percent of the total vote. These parties may have siphoned off some of the support in the urbanized areas that had previously gone to the long established leftist parties, namely, the Socialist and Communist. For instance, in Tokyo and Osaka (which together elect a total of seven representatives) the Communists elected one and the Socialists none. By contrast, the middle-of-the-road Clean Government and Democratic Socialist parties, both looked upon as potential coalition partners of the Liberal Democratic party, did better than in 1974. It is in the highly urbanized areas where dissatisfaction with the old parties is strong and where the number of people who refuse to commit themselves to any one party is fairly large, and it is in these areas that the new minor parties got some support. For example, the two best prefectures for the Socialist Citizens' League were Saitama and Kyoto, and the best for the United Progressive Liberals was Tokyo.

In any case, a coalition government, if and when it materializes, is certain to be more sensitive to urban interests than the Liberal Democratic party has been. The political system may respond slowly, but it does eventually respond. The question is whether it will respond quickly enough and in a way that will generally satisfy the electorate.

Obviously, the investment model, because it is a simplified representation of reality, cannot explain everything that happens. But it does provide an explanation for some important political developments. No doubt other analysts will be able to suggest alternative models that will explain the same phenomena in some other fashion. Eventually, when we have several competing models before us, we will be able to choose the most useful. The present investment model has been put forward in the hope that students of Japanese politics in particular, and of comparative politics in general, will eventually have access to a variety of models to assist in their analysis of democratic political systems and to help guide their research.

Notes

Introduction

1. Bradley Richardson, "Urbanization and Political Participation: The Case of Japan," *American Political Science Review* 67, no. 2 (June 1973): 436.

2. Chong Lim Kim, "Socio-economic Development and Political Democracy in Japanese Prefectures," *American Political Science Review* 65, no. 1 (March 1971): 186.

3. Gabriel Almond and Sidney Verba, *The Civic Culture* (Princeton, N.J.: Princeton University Press, 1963).

4. Giovanni Sartori, *Parties and Party Systems* (Cambridge: Cambridge University Press, 1976).

Chapter 1

1. C. B. Macpherson, *Democratic Theory: Essays in Retrieval* (Oxford: Clarendon Press, 1963), p. 51.

2. George De Vos, *Socialization for Achievement: Essays on the Cultural Psychology of the Japanese* (Berkeley: University of California Press, 1973), p. 196.

3. Macpherson, *Democratic Theory*, p. 185.

4. Anthony Downs, *An Economic Theory of Democracy* (New York: Harper and Row, 1957), p. 27.

5. Ibid., p. 37.

6. Ibid., p. 28.

7. Ibid., pp. 26-27.

8. Ibid., p. 11.

9. Ibid., p. 36.

10. Ibid., p. 36.

11. Ibid., p. 31.

12. Ibid., p. 88.

13. J. S. Sorzano, "David Easton and the Invisible Hand," *American Political Science Review* 69, no. 1 (March 1975): 98.

14. David Easton, *Systems Analysis of Political Life* (New York: Wiley, 1965), pp. 364-365.

15. Downs, *An Economic Theory*, p. 259.

16. Peter Blau, *Exchange and Power in Social Life* (New York: Wiley, 1964), p. 236.

17. Downs, *An Economic Theory*, p. 268.

18. Ibid., p. 270.

19. Brian Barry, *Sociologists, Economists and Democracy* (London: Collier-MacMillan, 1970), p. 20.

20. Samuel Popkin et al., "Comment: What Have You Done for Me Lately? Toward an Investment Theory of Voting," *American Political Science Review* 70, no. 3 (September 1976): 779-805.

21. Ibid., p. 786. Emphasis in original.

22. Ibid., p. 787.

23. Ibid.

24. See Downs, *An Economic Theory*, p. 16.

25. There are many examples in James White, *The Sokagakkai and Mass Society* (Stanford, Calif.: Stanford University Press, 1970), on the activities of the Sokagakkai, the parent organization of the Komeito. On the Communist party, see George Totten, "The People's Parliamentary Path of the Japanese Communist Party," pt. 2, *Pacific Affairs* 46, no. 3 (Autumn, 1973): 384-406; also H. N. Kim, "Deradicalization of the Japanese Communist Party under Kenji Miyamoto," *World Politics* 28, no. 2 (January 1976).

26. Bradley Richardon, *The Political Culture of Japan* (Berkeley: University of California Press, 1974), chapter 2.

Chapter 2

1. Carl Sheingold, "Social Networks and Voting: The Resurrection of Research Agenda," *American Sociological Review* 38 (December 1973): 712-720.

2. Bernard R. Berelson, Paul F. Lazarsfeld, and William N. McPhee, *Voting: A Study of Opinion Formation in a Presidential Campaign* (Chicago: University of Chicago Press, 1954), p. 94.

3. Ibid., p. 116.

4. Ibid., pp. 122-123.

5. Sheingold, "Social Networks," p. 718.

6. Martin Fitton, "Neighborhood and Voting: A Sociometric Examination," *British Journal of Political Science* 3, pt. 4 (October 1973): 472.

7. Paul Burstein, "Social Networks and Voting: Some Israeli Data," *Social Forces* 54, no. 4 (June 1976): 835.

8. Ibid., pp. 844-845.

9. Heinz Eulau, "Social Networks, Contextual Analysis and Electoral Behavior," November 1976, p. 3. An unpublished paper my colleague kindly made available to me. Quoted with his permission.

10. Ibid., p. 4.

11. Ibid., p. 6.

12. Chie Nakane, *Japanese Society* (Berkeley: University of California Press, 1970), p. x.

13. Ibid., p. 40.

14. See Luigi Graziano, "A Conceptual Framework for the Study of Clientelistic Behavior," *European Journal of Political Research* 4 (1976): 149-174. A fairly extensive list of titles may be found in his footnotes.

15. Nakane, *Japanese Society*, p. 31.

16. Ibid.

17. Ibid., pp. 70-71.

18. Ibid., p. 83.

19. Ibid., p. 121.

20. Ibid., pp. 59-60.

21. Ibid., p. 87.

22. Ibid., p. 102.

23. Ibid., p. 103.

24. Takeo Doi, *Amae no Kozo* [Structure of amae] (Tokyo, 1971).

25. De Vos, *Socialization for Achievement*, p 49.

26. Ibid.

27. Doi, *Amae*, pp. 82-83.

28. Nakane, *Japanese Society*, p. 65.

29. Ibid.

30. Doi, *Amae*, pp. 41 ff.

31. Ibid., pp. 94 ff.

32. Thomas P. Rohlen, *For Harmony and Strength: Japanese White-collar Organization in Anthropological Perspective* (Berkeley: University of California Press, 1974), p. 263.

33. Ibid., p. 264.
34. Ibid., p. 265.

Chapter 3

1. Mancur Olson, *The Logic of Collective Action* (Cambridge, Mass.: Harvard University Press, 1965), p. 13.
2. Dennis Mueller, "Public Choice: A Survey," *Journal of Economic Literature* 14, no. 2 (June 1976): 411.
3. Angus Campbell et al., *The American Voter*, abridged ed. (New York: Wiley, 1964), pp. 1, 177.
4. Graziano, "A Conceptual Framework," p. 157.
5. Ibid., p. 158.
6. Peter Ekeh, *Social Exchange: The Two Traditions* (Cambridge, Mass.: Harvard University Press, 1974), p. 205.
7. Graziano, "A Conceptual Framework," p. 159.
8. *Yomiuri Shimbun*, December 7, 1976.
9. Robert Lane, *Political Thinking and Consciousness* (Chicago: Markham Publishing Co., 1966), pp. 302-303.
10. Richard Solomon, *Mao's Revolution and the Chinese Political Culture* (Berkeley: University of California Press, 1971).
11. Ibid., p. 149.
12. Ibid., pp. 144, 135.
13. Tokeisuri Kenkyujo, *Kenminsei no Tokei-teki Kenkyu* [Statistical study of prefectural characteristics] (Tokyo, 1972), pp. 67-71.
14. James Q. Wilson, *Political Organizations* (New York: Basic Books, 1973), p. 21.
15. Nakane, *Japanese Society*, pp. 59-60.
16. Ibid.
17. *Asahi Shimbun*, December 8, 1976.
18. Nakane, *Japanese Society*, p. 60.
19. Maruyama Masao, "Patterns of Individuation and the Case of Japan; A Conceptual Scheme," in *Changing Japanese Attitudes Towards Modernization*, ed. Marius Jansen (Princeton, N.J.: Princeton University Press, 1965), pp. 489-531; Okuda Michio, "Jumin Ishiki to Gyosei Juyo" [Views of residents and administrative demands] in *Toshi Shakai no Keisei no Ronri to Jumin* [Logic of the formation of urban society and its residents], ed. Isomura Eiichi (Tokyo, 1971), pp. 135-177.
20. Kurasawa Susumu, ed., *Toshi Shakaigaku* [Urban sociology], *Shakaigaku koza* [Series on sociology], vol. 5 (Tokyo, 1973), pp. 146-147.
21. In a 1969-1970 survey in Hachioji, a satellite city of Tokyo,

respondents were classified into these four categories on the basis of their responses to a set of questions. Respondents were asked, among other things, to state which political parties they supported. Those in category 1 (dependency) inclined toward the Liberal Democratic party, and those in category 2 (apathetic) tended to be in the not-voting category or favored the Liberal Democrats. Those in category 3 (privatized) were more spread out among the various parties, with a tendency to favor the Liberal Democrats, the Socialists, and the Communists. Finally, respondents in category 4 (civic-minded) were also spread out, mostly among the Liberal Democrats and Socialists, but with some tendency toward the Democratic Socialists and Communists. See Okuda, "Jumin Ishiki," pp. 141-145. Additional data on Kobe and Takarazuka may be found in Tanaka Kunio, "Shimin Seiji Ishiki no Hensen ni Kansuru Bunseki" [An analysis of changes in citizen political attitudes], *Toshi Seisaku*, no. 5 (October 1976), pp. 106-107.

22. James White, *Political Implications of Cityward Migration; Japan as an Exploratory Test Case*, Sage Publications, Comparative Politics series, no. 01-038 (Beverly Hills: Sage Publications, 1973), pp. 28 ff.

23. Isomura, *Toshi Shakai*, p. 399.

24. Nakane, *Japanese Society*, p. 21.

25. Seymour M. Lipset and Reinhard Bendix, *Social Mobility in Industrial Society* (Berkeley: University of California Press, 1959), p. 70.

26. Nakane, *Japanese Society*, p. 1.

27. Nihon Hoso Kyokai, Hoso Seron Chosajo, *Nihonjin no Ishiki* [Attitudes of the Japanese] (Tokyo, 1975), p. 380.

28. George Homans, *The Human Group* (New York: Harcourt, Brace, 1950), p.120.

29. Nakane, *Japanese Society*, p. 29.

30. Sidney Verba, *Small Groups and Political Behavior* (Princeton, N.J.: Princeton University Press, 1961), p. 151.

31. Ibid., chapter 6.

32. De Vos, *Socialization for Achievement*, p. 33.

33. Verba, *Small Groups*, p. 149.

34. Ibid., p. 172.

35. Ibid., p. 222.

36. Downs, *An Economic Theory*, p. 28.

37. Ibid., p. 24.

38. Robert Dahl, *A Preface to Democratic Theory* (Chicago: University of Chicago Press, 1956), p. 124.

39. Ibid., p. 132.

40. For a discussion of political trust, see Kohei Shinsaku and Matsushima Kei, "Seiji Fushin no Ishiki Kozo" [Attitudinal structure of political distrust], *Bunken Geppo,* July 1976.

41. J. P. Nettl, *Political Mobilization: A Sociological Analysis of Methods and Concepts* (New York: Basic Books, 1967), pp. 374-375.

42. Ibid., p. 351.

43. Ibid., p. 357.

44. Rohlen, *For Harmony and Strength,* pp. 263-265.

45. Nakane, *Japanese Society,* p. 38.

Chapter 4

1. Morris Janowitz and David Segal, "Social Cleavage and Party Affiliation; Germany, Great Britain, and the United States," in *Mass Politics in Industrial Societies,* ed. Giuseppe Di Palma (Chicago: Markham, 1972), pp. 201 ff.

2. Ibid., pp. 201-202.

3. Heinz Eulau, *Class and Party in the Eisenhower Years* (Glencoe, Ill.: Free Press, 1962), p. 141. Janowitz and Segal, "Social Cleavage," also discuss this model.

4. Joji Watanuki, "Patterns of Politics in Present-day Japan," in *Party Systems and Voter Alignments,* ed. Seymour M. Lipset and Stein Rokkan (New York: Free Press, 1967), pp. 447-466.

5. Ibid., p. 457.

6. Ibid., p. 454.

7. De Vos, *Socialization for Achievement,* p. 13.

8. Ibid., p. 60.

9. Frank Parkin, "Working Class Conservatism: A Theory of Political Deviance," *British Journal of Sociology* 18 (1967): 279.

10. Ibid., p. 282.

11. Tokeisuri Kenkyujo, *Dai-2 Nihonjin no Kokuminsei* [Japanese national character, volume 2] (Tokyo, 1970), pp. 207-211; see also Hayashi Chikio's remarks in Nihonjin Kenkyukai, ed., *Shiji Seito-betsu Nihonjin Shudan* [Japanese groups and party support], *Nihonjin Kenkyu,* series 2 (Tokyo, 1975), p. 54.

12. Robert Alford, "Class Voting in the Anglo-American Political Systems," in Lipset and Rokkan, *Party Systems,* p. 80.

13. Ikeuchi Hajime et al., *Shimin Ishiki no Kenkyu* [A study of citizen attitudes] (Tokyo, 1974), p. 427.

14. Based on data in Tokeisuri Kenkyujo, *Kokuminsei no Kenkyu* [Study of national character], 1968 (Tokyo, 1969), p. 143.

15. Sodei Takako, "Keizai Seicho to Shakai Seiso no Henka"

[Economic growth and changes in social stratification], *Nihon Rodo Kyokai Zasshi* 15, no. 6 (June 1973): 12.

16. Ellis Krauss, *Japanese Radicals Revisited* (Berkeley: University of California Press, 1974).

17. Ibid., p. 46.

18. Ibid., p. 48.

19. Ibid., p. 53.

20. Ibid., p. 49.

21. Nakamura Kikuo, ed., *Nihon ni okeru Seito to Seiji Ishiki* [Political parties in Japan and political attitudes] (Tokyo, 1971).

22. Ibid., pp. 44-45.

23. Ibid., pp. 109-111, 132.

24. Ibid., p. 109.

25. Hashimoto Akikazu, *Shiji Seito Nashi* [Support no party] (Tokyo, 1975), p. 72.

26. Miyake Ichiro et al., *Kotonaru Reberu no Senkyo ni okeru Tohyo Kodo no Kenkyu* [Study of electoral behavior in elections at various levels] (Tokyo, 1967).

27. Ibid., p. 118.

28. Ibid., p. 117.

Chapter 5

1. Norman Nie and Sidney Verba, "Political Participation," in *Handbook of Political Science,* ed. Fred Greenstein and Nelson Polsby, vol. 4 (Reading, Mass.: Addison-Wesley, 1975), p. 33.

2. Ibid., p. 35.

3. Both Nathaniel Thayer, *How the Conservatives Rule Japan* (Princeton, N.J.: Princeton University Press, 1969); and Gerald Curtis, *Campaigning Japanese Style* (New York: Columbia University Press, 1971) provide numerous examples of mobilization.

4. Miyakawa Takayoshi, ed., *Seiji Handobukku* [Political handbook] (Tokyo, 1976), pp. 288-289.

5. *Sankei,* December 7, 1976.

6. Aiba Jun-ichi, "Seinen no Seiji Ishiki" [Political attitudes of youth], *Shakaigaku Hyoron* 22 (December 1971): 17.

7. Maruyama, "Patterns of Individuation," p. 494.

8. Robert J. Lifton, "Youth and History," *Asian Cultural Studies,* no. 3 (October 1962), p. 125.

9. Nobutaka Ike, "Economic Growth and Intergenerational Change in Japan," *American Political Science Review* 67, no. 4 (December 1973): 1194-1203.

10. Maruyama, "Patterns of Individuation," p. 498.

11. Shiratori Rei, *Seron, Senkyo, Seiji* [Public opinion, elections, and politics] (Tokyo, 1972); also Kohei Shinsaku, "Taisei Sentaku no Seiji Ishiki" [Systematic choice and political attitudes], *Bunken Geppo*, November 1974, pp. 3-4.

12. Nakamura Kei-ichi, "Datsu Seito-ka Gensho ni Tsuite" [On the no-party phenomenon], *Senkyo* 25 (August 1972): 14-26.

13. Kohei, "Taisei Sentaku," p. 14.

Chapter 6

1. Shiratori, *Seron*, pp. 38-39.

2. Nishihira Shigeki, "Naze Minobe wa Katta ka" [Why did Minobe win?], *Jiyu*, June 1971, p. 123.

3. Taketsugu Tsurutani, "A New Era in Japanese Politics: Tokyo Gubernatorial Elections," *Asian Survey* 12 (May 1972): 430.

4. Ibid., p. 441.

5. Samuel Beer et al., *Patterns of Government*, 2d ed. (New York: Random House, 1972), p. 117.

6. Nishihira, "Naze Minobe," p. 124.

7. K. Kuwata, "Lessons of the General Local Elections," *Japan Quarterly* 18 (July-September 1971): 280.

8. Nishihira, "Naze Minobe," p. 122.

9. Shiratori, *Seron*, p. 57.

10. Kuwata, "Lessons," p. 275.

11. "Tokyo-to-min no Tohyo Kodo" [Electoral behavior of Tokyo residents], *Naikaku Chosashitsu Chosa Geppo*, no. 194 (February 1972), pp. 54-55.

12. Okubo Sadayoshi, "Tomin no Tohyo Kodo to Seiji Ishiki" [Political consciousness and voting behavior of Tokyo residents], *Senkyo* 24 (June 1971): 8.

13. Shiratori, *Seron*, p. 33.

14. See "Tokyo-to-min no Tohyo Kodo," p. 43.

15. Kohei Shinsaku, "Tato-ka Gensho to Fudohyo" [Multiparty phenomenon and the floating vote], Nihon Hoso Kyokai, Hoso Seron Kenkyujo, August 1969, p. 2.

16. Shinohara Hajime, "Henyosuru Nihon no Seiji Fudo" [Japan's changing political climate], *Asahi Journal* 13, no. 16 (April 2, 1971): 126.

17. Nihon Hoso Kyokai, Hoso Seron Chosajo, *Nihonjin no Ishiki*, p. 67.

18. Kita Ei-ichiro, "Datsu Seitoka Gensho to Shimin Undo"

[No-party phenomenon and citizens' movements], *Senkyo* 24 (October 1971); Shiratori, *Seron,* pp. 97 ff.

19. Joseph Massey, "The Missing Leader: Japanese Youths' View of Political Authority," *American Political Science Review* 69, no. 1 (March 1975): 40-41.

20. Ibid., p. 41.

21. Shiratori, *Seron,* p. 34; "Tokyo-to Chiji Senkyo no Bunseki" [Analysis of the Tokyo gubernatorial election], *Naikaku Chosashitsu Chosa Geppo,* no. 238 (October 1975), p. 39.

22. Hashimoto, *Shiji Seito,* pp. 22, 98.

23. Ibid., p. 9. (These are inferences I have made from Hashimoto's poll data.)

24. See Kokumin Senkodo Chosa Iinkai, ed., *Nihonjin no Manzokudo* [How satisfied are the Japanese?] (Tokyo, 1972), which gives data as of 1971 for four localities including Tokyo.

Chapter 7

1. V. O. Key, Jr., *Southern Politics* (New York: Random House, 1949), pp. 39-40.

2. Ibid., p. 37.

3. Ibid., p. 41.

4. Ibid., p. 38.

5. Ibid.

6. Ibid., p. 37.

7. Additional examples can be found in Curtis, *Campaigning,* chapter 4; Thayer, *Conservatives,* pp. 98 ff; and Nihonjin Kenkyukai, ed., *Shiji Seito,* pp. 207-264.

8. Jack Lewis, "Hokaku Rengo: The Politics of Conservative-Progressive Cooperation in a Japanese City" (Ph.D. diss., Stanford University, 1974), p. 155.

9. J. A. A. Stockwin, *Japan; Divided Politics in a Growth Economy* (New York: Norton, 1975), p. 157.

10. James Coleman, *Introduction to Mathematical Sociology* (Glencoe, Ill.: Free Press, 1964), p. 272.

11. Ibid.

12. Ibid., p. 275.

13. Tomita Nobuo, "Jimoto Ishiki no Bunseki" [Analysis of localism], in *Shiji Seito,* ed. Nihonjin Kenkyukai, pp. 218-219.

14. *Asahi Shimbun,* December 7, 1976.

15. Ibid.

16. *Sankei Shimbun,* December 6, 1976.

17. Popkin et al., "Comment," pp. 794-795.

Bibliography

Aiba, Jun-ichi. "Seinen no Seiji Ishiki" [Political attitudes of Japanese youth]. *Shakaigaku Hyoron* 22 (December 1971).

Almond, Gabriel, and Verba, Sidney. *The Civic Culture.* Princeton, N.J.: Princeton University Press, 1963.

Barry, Brian. *Sociologists, Economists and Democracy.* London: Collier-MacMillan, 1970.

Beer, Samuel, et al. *Patterns of Government.* 2d ed. New York: Random House, 1972.

Berelson, Bernard; Lazarsfeld, Paul; and McPhee, William. *Voting: A Study of Opinion Formation in a Presidential Campaign.* Chicago: University of Chicago Press, 1954.

Blalock, Hubert, Jr. *Theory Construction: From Verbal to Mathematical Formulations.* Englewood Cliffs, N.J.: Prentice-Hall, 1969.

Blau, Peter. *Exchange and Power in Social Life.* New York: Wiley, 1964.

Burstein, Paul. "Social Networks and Voting; Some Israeli Data." *Social Forces* 54 (June 1976).

Campell, Angus; Converse, Philip E.; Miller, Warren; and Stokes, Donald. *The American Voter.* New York: Wiley, 1960. Abridged edition.

Coleman, James. *Introduction to Mathematical Sociology.* Glencoe, Ill.: Free Press, 1964.

Curtis, Gerald. *Campaigning Japanese Style.* New York: Columbia University Press, 1971.

Dahl, Robert. *A Preface to Democratic Theory.* Chicago: University of Chicago Press, 1956.

———. *Polyarchy: Participation and Opposition.* New Haven: Yale University Press, 1971.

De Vos, George. *Socialization for Achievement: Essays on the Cultural Psychology of the Japanese.* Berkeley: University of California Press, 1973.

Doi, Takeo. *Amae no Kozo* [Structure of amae]. Tokyo, 1971.

Downs, Anthony. *An Economic Theory of Democracy.* New York: Harper and Row, 1957.

Easton, David. *Systems Analysis of Political Life.* New York: Wiley, 1965.

Ekeh, Peter. *Social Exchange: The Two Traditions.* Cambridge, Mass.: Harvard University Press, 1974.

Eulau, Heinz. *Class and Party in the Eisenhower Years.* Glencoe, Ill.: Free Press, 1962.

———. "Social Networks, Contextual Analysis and Electoral Behavior." 1976. An unpublished essay.

Fitton, Martin. "Neighborhood and Voting; A Sociometric Examination." *British Journal of Political Science* 3 (October 1973).

Flanagan, Scott. "The Japanese Party System in Transition." *Comparative Politics* (January 1971).

Graziano, Luigi. "A Conceptual Framework for the Study of Clientelistic Behavior." *European Journal of Political Research* 4 (1976).

Hashimoto, Akikazu. *Shiji Seito Nashi* [Support no party]. Tokyo, 1975.

Homans, George. *The Human Group.* New York: Harcourt, Brace, 1950.

Ike, Nobutaka. "Economic Growth and Intergenerational Change in Japan." *American Political Science Review* 67 (December 1973).

Ikeuchi, Hajime, et al. *Shimin Ishiki no Kenkyu* [A study of citizen attitudes]. Tokyo, 1974.

Isomura, Ei-ichi, ed. *Toshi Shakai Keisei no Ronri to Jumin* [Logic of the formation of urban society and its residents]. Tokyo, 1971.

Janowitz, Morris, and Segal, David. "Social Cleavage and Party Affiliation: Germany, Great Britain, and the United States." In *Mass Politics in Industrial Societies.* Edited by Giuseppi Di Palma. Chicago: Markham Publishing Co., 1972.

Katz, Elihu, and Lazarsfeld, Paul. *Personal Influence: The Part Played by People in the Flow of Mass Communications.* New

York: Free Press, 1955.

Key, V. O., Jr. *Southern Politics.* New York: Random House, 1949.

Kim, Chong Lim. "Socio-economic Development and Political Democracy in Japanese Prefectures." *American Political Science Review* 65 (March 1971).

Kim, H. N. "Deradicalization of the Japanese Communist Party under Kenji Miyamoto." *World Politics* 28 (January 1976.)

Kita, Ei-ichiro. "Datsu Seitoka Gensho to Shimin Undo" [No party phenomenon and citizens' movements]. *Senkyo* 24 (October 1971).

Kohei, Shinsaku. "Dai 34-kai Shugiin Senkyo ni Miru Kokumin no Seiji Ishiki" [Political attitudes of the people in the 34th House of Representatives election]. *Bunken Geppo,* February 1977.

_____. "Taisei Sentaku no Seiji Ishiki" [Systemic choice and political attitudes]. *Bunken Geppo,* November 1974.

_____. and Matsushita, Kei. "Seiji Fushin no Ishiki Kozo" [Attitudinal structure of political distrust]. *Bunken Geppo,* July 1976.

_____. "Tato-ka Gensho to Fudohyo" [Multiparty phenomenon and the floating vote]. Nihon Hoso Kyokai, Hoso Seron Kenkyujo, August 1969.

Kokumin Senkodo Chosa Iin-kai, ed. *Nihonjin no Manzokudo* [How satisfied are the Japanese?]. Tokyo, 1972.

Krauss, Ellis. *Japanese Radicals Revisited.* Berkeley: University of California Press, 1974.

Kurosawa, Susumu, ed. *Toshi Shakaigaku* [Urban sociology]. *Shakaigaku Koza* [Series on sociology] 5. Tokyo, 1973.

Kuwata, K. "Lessons of the General Local Elections." *Japan Quarterly* 18 (July-September 1971).

Lane, Robert. *Political Thinking and Consciousness.* Chicago: Markham Publishing Co., 1966.

Lewis, Jack. "Hokaku Rengo: The Politics of Conservative-Progressive Cooperation in a Japanese City." Ph.D. dissertation Stanford University, 1974.

Lifton, Robert. "Youth and History." *Asian Cultural Studies* No. 3 (October 1962).

Lipset, Seymour M., and Rokkan, Stein. *Party Systems and Voter Alignments.* New York: Free Press, 1967.

_____, and Bendix, Reinhard. *Social Mobility in Industrial*

Society. Berkeley: University of California Press, 1959.

Macpherson, C. B. *Democratic Theory; Essays in Retrieval.* Oxford: Clarendon Press, 1963.

Maruyama, Masao. "Patterns of Individuation and the Case of Japan; A Conceptual Scheme." In *Changing Japanese Attitudes towards Modernization*. Edited by Marius Jansen. Princeton, N.J.: Princeton University Press, 1965.

Massey, Joseph. "The Missing Leader: Japanese Youths' View of Political Authority." *American Political Science Review* 69 (March 1975).

Miyakawa, Takayoshi, ed. *Seiji Handobukku* [Political handbook]. Tokyo, 1976.

Miyake, Ichiro, et al. *Kotonaru Reberu no Senkyo ni okeru Tohyo Kodo no Kenkyu* [Study of electoral behavior in elections at various levels]. Tokyo, 1967.

Mueller, Dennis. "Public Choice; A Survey." *Journal of Economic Literature* 14 (June 1976).

Nakane, Chie. *Japanese Society*. Berkeley: University of California Press, 1970.

Nakamura, Kei-ichi. "Datsu Seito-ka Gensho ni Tsuite" [On the no-party phenomenon]. *Senkyo* 25 (August 1972).

Nakamura, Kikuo, ed. *Nihon ni okeru Seito to Seiji Ishiki* [Political parties in Japan and political attitudes]. Tokyo, 1971.

Naoi, Atsushi, et el. *Hendoki no Nihon Shakai* [Japanese society in a period of change]. Tokyo, 1972.

Nettl, J. P. *Political Mobilization; A Sociological Analysis of Methods and Concepts*. New York: Basic Books, 1967.

Nie, Norman, and Verba, Sidney. "Political Participation." In *Handbook of Political Science* 4. Edited by Fred Greenstein and Nelson Polsby. Reading, Mass.: Addison-Wesley, 1975.

Nihon Hoso Kyokai, Hoso Seron Chosajo. *Nihonjin no Ishiki* [Attitudes of the Japanese]. Tokyo, 1975.

Nihonjin Kenkyukai, ed. *Shiji Seito-betsu Nihonjin Shudan* [Japanese groups and party support], *Nihonjin Kenkyu* Series 2. Tokyo, 1975.

Nishihara, Shigeki. "Naze Minobe wa Katta Ka" [Why did Minobe win?]. *Jiyu,* June 1971.

Okazaki, Yoichi. "Saikin ni okeru Jinko Rodo no Chiiki-teki Bumpu no Henka ni Tsuite" [On the regional distribution of the labor force in recent times]. *Nihon Rodo Kyokai Zasshi*, no. 170 (May 1970).

Okubo, Sadayoshi. "Tomin no Tohyo Kodo to Seiji Ishiki"

[Political consciousness and voting behavior of Tokyo residents]. *Senkyo* 24 (April, June 1971).

Olson, Mancur. *The Logic of Collective Action*. Cambridge, Mass.: Harvard University Press, 1965.

Parkin, Frank. "Working Class Conservatism; A Theory of Political Deviance." *British Journal of Sociology* 18 (1967).

Popkin, Samuel; Gorman, John W.; Phillips, Charles; and Smith, Jeffrey A. "Comment: What Have You Done for Me Lately? Toward An Investment Theory of Voting." *American Political Science Review* 70 (September 1976).

Richardson, Bradley. *The Political Culture of Japan*. Berkeley: University of California Press, 1974.

———. "Urbanization and Political Participation: The Case of Japan." *American Political Science Review* 67 (June 1973).

Rohlen, Thomas. *For Harmony and Strength: Japanese White-collar Organization in Anthropological Perspective*. Berkeley: University of California Press, 1974.

Sartori, Giovanni. *Parties and Party Systems*. Cambridge: Cambridge University Press, 1976.

Sheingold, Carl. "Social Networks and Voting; The Resurrection of Research Agenda." *American Sociological Review* 38 (December 1973).

Shinohara, Hajime. "Henyosuru Nihon no Seiji Fudo" [Japan's changing political climate]. *Asahi Journal* 13 (April 2, 1971).

Shiratori, Rei. *Seron, Senkyo, Seiji* [Public opinion, elections, and politics]. Tokyo, 1972.

Sodei, Takako. "Keizai Seicho no Shakai Seiso no Henka" [Economic growth and changes in social stratification]. *Nihon Rodo Kyokai Zasshi* 15 (June 1973).

Solomon, Richard. *Mao's Revolution and the Chinese Political Culture*. Berkeley: University of California Press, 1971.

Sorzano, J. S. "David Easton and the Invisible Hand." *American Political Science Review* 69 (March 1975).

Stockwin, J. A. A. *Japan: Divided Politics in a Growth Economy*. New York: Norton, 1975.

Tanaka, Kunio. "Shimin Seiji Ishiki no Hensen ni Kansuru Bunseki" [Analysis of changes in political attitudes among urban dwellers]. *Toshi Seisaku* no. 5 (October 1976).

Thayer, Nathaniel. *How Conservatives Rule Japan*. Princeton, N.J.: Princeton University Press, 1969.

Tokeisuri Kenkyujo. *Dai-2 Nihonjin no Kokuminsei* [Japanese national character, volume 2]. Tokyo, 1970.

_____. *Kenminsei no Tokei-teki Kenkyu* [Statistical study of prefectural characteristics]. Tokyo, 1972.

_____. *Kokuminsei no Kenkyu, 1968* [Study of national character]. Tokyo, 1969.

"Tokyo-to-min no Tohyo Kodo" [Electoral behavior of Tokyo Residents]. *Naikaku Chosashitsu Chosa Geppo* no. 194 [February 1972).

Totten, George. "The People's Parliamentary Path of the Japanese Communist Party, Part II." *Pacific Affairs* 46 (Fall 1973).

Tsurutani, Taketsugu. "A New Era in Japanese Politics; Tokyo Gubernatorial Elections." *Asian Survey* 12 (May, 1972).

_____. *Political Change in Japan.* New York: McKay, 1977.

Tufte, Edward. *Data Analysis for Politics and Policy.* Englewood Cliffs, N.J.: Prentice-Hall, 1974.

Verba, Sidney. *Small Groups and Political Behavior.* Princeton, N.J.: Princeton University Press, 1961.

White, James. *Political Implications of Cityward Migration; Japan as an Exploratory Test Case.* Beverly Hills: Sage Publications, 1973.

_____. *The Sokagakkai and Mass Society.* Stanford: Stanford University Press, 1970.

Wilson, James. *Political Organizations.* New York: Basic Books, 1973.

Yasuda Saburo. *Gendai Nihon no Kaikyu Ishiki* [Class consciousness in contemporary Japan]. Tokyo, 1973.

Yomiuri Shimbun. *Senkyo o Tettei Bunsekisuru* [A thorough analysis of elections]. Tokyo, 1975.

Zetterberg, Hans. *On Theory and Verification in Sociology.* Totowa, N.J.: Bedminster Press, 1965.

Index